FORTRESS
SINGAPORE

THE BATTLEFIELD GUIDE

Carnage after one of the initial bombings on Singapore.

By
Maj. Yap Siang Yong
Romen Bose
Angeline Pang
Kuldip Singh
Lisa Lim
Germaine Foo

Marshall Cavendish Editions

Researched by Vijayan, Leslie Tan, Marc Lee, Tania Low-Tan Lay Hwa,
Ho Cheun Hon, Lisa Lim, Germaine Foo and Vickna S K Anandarajah.

Cover design by Lock Hong Liang
Images of Spitfire on cover by Byron Hardy (byronh1/SXC.hu) and
Philip MacKenzie (bugdog/SXC.hu)
Site maps by Benson Tan

© 1992 Ministry of Defence, Singapore
Second edition 1995, Third edition 2003
© Fourth edition 2004, Marshall Cavendish International (Asia) Private Limited
Reprinted 2005, 2011 (with new cover), 2016

Published by Marshall Cavendish Editions
An imprint of Marshall Cavendish International
1 New Industrial Road, Singapore 536196

All rights reserved

No part of this publication may be reproduced, stored in a retrieval system or transmitted, in any form or by any means, electronic, mechanical, photocopying, recording or otherwise, without the prior permission of the copyright owner. Request for permission should be addressed to the Publisher, Marshall Cavendish International (Asia) Private Limited, 1 New Industrial Road, Singapore 536196. Tel: (65) 6213 9300, fax: (65) 6285 4871. E-mail: genrefsales@sg.marshallcavendish.com. Website: www.marshallcavendish.com/genref

The publisher makes no representation or warranties with respect to the contents of this book, and specifically disclaims any implied warranties or merchantability or fitness for any particular purpose, and shall in no event be liable for any loss of profit or any other commercial damage, including but not limited to special, incidental, consequential, or other damages.

Other Marshall Cavendish Offices

Marshall Cavendish Corporation. 99 White Plains Road, Tarrytown NY 10591-9001, USA • Marshall Cavendish International (Thailand) Co Ltd. 253 Asoke, 12th Flr, Sukhumvit 21 Road, Klongtoey Nua, Wattana, Bangkok 10110, Thailand • Marshall Cavendish (Malaysia) Sdn Bhd, Times Subang, Lot 46, Subang Hi-Tech Industrial Park, Batu Tiga, 40000 Shah Alam, Selangor Darul Ehsan, Malaysia

Marshall Cavendish is a trademark of Times Publishing Limited

National Library Board Singapore Cataloguing in Publication Data

Fortress Singapore : the battlefield guide / by Yap Siang Yong ... [et al.].
– Singapore : Marshall Cavendish Editions, 2011.
p. cm.
Includes bibliographical references.
ISBN : 978-981-4351-19-5 (pbk.)

1. Singapore – History – Siege, 1942. 2. World War, 1939-1945 – Singapore.
3. World War, 1939-1945 – Battlefields – Singapore – Guidebooks.
4. Historic sites – Singapore – Guidebooks. 5. Singapore – Tours. I. Yap, Siang Yong.

D767.55
959.5703—dc22   OCN710971280

Printed in Singapore by Markono Print Media Pte Ltd

The remnants of the Royal Air Force flying up north to defend the besieged peninsula.

Fortress Singapore

Contents

Introduction 6
The Rising Sun 8
The Malayan Campaign 10
The Japanese Occupation 24
Allied Victory 32

The Northwestern Tour 37

N1 Kranji Reservoir Park 38
N2 Sarimbun Beach Battle Site 42
N3 Kranji War Memorial 46
N4 Bukit Batok Hilltop 50
N5 Ford Motor Factory 54
N6 Bukit Timah Battle 58

The Central Tour 63

C1 Kent Ridge Park 64
C2 Labrador Park 68
C3 Alexandra Hospital 70
C4 Singapore General Hospital 74

Contents

C5 Padang & City Hall *78*

C6 Kandahar Street *82*

C7 Fort Canning Park *86*

C8 Fort Siloso *88*

The Eastern Tour *93*

E1 Changi Prison *94*

E2 Selarang Barracks *98*

E3 Johore Battery *102*

E4 Changi Murals *106*

Other Memorials *110*

WWII Plaques and Historic Sites *115*

The Military Museums *121*

M1 RSN Museum *122*

M2 RSAF Museum *124*

Selected Bibliography *127*

Fortress Singapore

Introduction

*15 February, 1942.
The strongest British bastion east of Suez, falls to the Empire of the Rising Sun, after only 70 days.*

The Mail, Feb 16, 1942

This and many other headlines greeted shocked readers all over the world on 16 February 1942. The "impregnable fortress," with its massive fortifications and fixed batteries, and defended by over 100,000 men, fell to the conquering Japanese forces in only a week.

During the struggle for Singapore, desperate battles were fought throughout the island, and many of these battle sites remain today. As the Japanese army swept down the peninsula, hasty defences were set up to protect our northern shores. These northern sites still have that sense of urgency which gripped the island just before the invasion more than 50 years ago.

For the men and women who had fought so feverishly, the Japanese Occupation brought untold terror and hardships. Sirens, bombs, massacres, epidemics, shortages, concentration camps and POW centres were part of everyday life. The sites you will be visiting today capture the essence of what Singapore was like during those dark years when all one had left was faith, and a will to survive at all cost.

Though what remains today are but empty shells and lingering shadows, it is through understanding what happened here that these sites come alive again, never letting us forget the brutalities of war, and the faith and the inspiration of the people that laid the foundations of modern Singapore.

Maj. Yap Siang Yong
Romen Bose
Angeline Pang

Introduction

Photo Credits: Abdul Wahab, *Medical Students During The Japanese Invasion of Singapore, 1941–1942*; Archives and Oral History Department, Singapore; Aspinall, George, 1991, *Changi Photographer: George Aspinall's Record of Captivity,* Singapore: Times Editions; Australian War Memorial; Bose, Romen; Chuang Hui Tsuan Collection; Imperial War Museum, London; *Mainichi Shimbun*, Tokyo; Military Heritage Branch, Ministry of Defence, Singapore; Ministry of Information and the Arts, Singapore; On, Betty; Pang, Angeline; Ramsey, Winston G., *After The Battle*; Republic of Singapore Air Force; Republic of Singapore Navy, Naval Museum; Sentosa Wax Museum; Sheares, Major

The Rising Sun

Until the early 1800s, Japan had shut her doors to the outside world to prevent corrupting her people from foreign influences. This was to change in 1853, when American war ships forced themselves into her harbour and demanded that she open herself for trade.

The awesome display of technology in war, and the imposed system of trade from the West, made Japanese leaders realise that they would have to modernise and industrialise to beat the Western powers at their own game. If not, Japan would share the same fate as China whose territories were divided by Western imperialists. Four powerful clans from western Japan overthrew the Shogun who was blamed for failing to expel the foreigners. They rallied around the Emperor to restore his power in 1868 and created a central administration to carry out an ambitious modernisation programme.

As she grew in strength, Japan turned ambitious and wanted to expand her borders for more trade and the acquisition of raw materials for her industries. She defeated China in 1894 with her modern weapons and surprised the West by defeating Russia in 1905. Korea fell to her a few years later. In World War I, she wrested Qingdao, a port in China, from the Germans. She showed the world that she was the most powerful country in the East.

Events moving in the West were to aid Japan's expansionist plans. Germany invaded Austria in 1938 and advanced into Czechoslovakia a year later. When Hitler's tanks rolled into Poland in September 1939, Britain declared war on Germany. This was the start of World War II with France, Luxembourg, Belgium, Holland, Norway, Yugoslavia and Greece joining Britain to form the Allies against Germany and later, Italy.

Japan joined in with Germany and Italy to form the Axis Powers in 1940. In Europe, one by one, the other Allied countries fell into German hands. Even France, Britain's strongest Allied partner, surrendered to Germany in 1940. Britain was thus left to face the might of Germany and Italy alone. Britain gained another ally in Russia after the German invasion in 1941. She was also joined by the Americans in 1941 after Japan's attack on Pearl Harbour.

Japan, with similar expansionist plans as the Germans, advanced into China in July 1937 for her vast reserves of coal and iron, and her lucrative markets. It was to be a long war, and Japan decided to turn her attentions to Southeast Asia and the Pacific. With France

The Rising Sun

out of the picture, Japan advanced into French Indo-China. This worried the Americans who warned Japan to move out from Indo-China and to stop her aggression on China.

The U.S. and other European countries wanted China to remain free as they had special trading rights and exclusive trading zones through treaties with the Imperial Ching government. If Japan were to conquer China, it would abrogate existing treaties and remove the rights of these countries to trade in China. So when Japan refused to stop her war, the Americans, British and Dutch stopped the sale of war materials (oil, iron, rubber, tin, etc.) to Japan.

These essential supplies, however, were plentiful in Southeast Asia. And with the colonial masters of Southeast Asia busily occupied in their own wars — France and Holland were defeated by the Germans — Indo-China and the Dutch East Indies were open to Japanese occupation. Britain was too busy defending herself against Germany and Italy to protect her Southeast Asian territories. These events cleared the way for power-hungry Japan to step in.

But the Japanese had to contend with the Americans in the Pacific who had a formidable navy, army and air force strong enough to stop the Japanese. In order to prevent American interference in her march into Southeast Asia, Japan decided to attack Pearl Harbour — an important American naval base in Honolulu — on 7 December 1941, hoping to destroy the U.S. Pacific fleet. Their ploy, however, did not succeed as Japan's main targets, the aircraft carriers, were out at sea. The attack, though, succeeded in bombing most of the battleships and planes at Pearl Harbour. Japanese planes also destroyed the American air force stationed in the Philippines. Around 2,400 Americans were killed in the historic attack on Pearl Harbour. The United States was thus brought into the war on the side of the Allies.

The underlying propaganda behind Japan's conquest of Southeast Asia was her aim to create an "Asia for the Asiatics" and a "Greater East Asian Co-Prosperity Sphere." She made false promises of liberating Southeast Asia from their colonial masters and providing aid for their future development. In actual fact, Japan wanted only the rich resources of Southeast Asia for her industries and land for her expanding population. "Liberation" from the colonial masters only meant coming under the suppressive rule of the Japanese.

The Malayan Campaign

While Pearl Harbour was under attack at 3.25 am on 8 December 1941 (Tokyo time), the Japanese 25th Army's 18th Division had already landed at Kota Bahru at 2.15 am. Another Japanese Division, the 5th, landed in Singora and Patani in southern Thailand at 4 am. The Japanese landings at Kota Bahru were met with stiff resistance. These landings marked the start of the Malayan campaign, Japan's planned conquest of Malaya.

The Japanese plan was to capture Singapore, where the British Naval Base and the army HQ for Malaya were situated.

On the same day, 17 Japanese navy bombers flying from Saigon (Ho Chi Minh City), attacked Keppel Harbour Docks, the Naval Base, Tengah and Seletar airbases in Singapore.

At dusk, the `Prince of Wales` and the `Repulse`, Singapore's main sea defence strength, also known as Force Z, left for their ill-fated journey to intercept the Japanese landings in Malaya, a trip which left more than 800 dead and the two ships sunk.

By 25 Dec, the Japanese had seized all Malayan territory lying north and west of the Perak River. This included Penang, Perlis, Kedah, Kelantan and a greater part of Perak. They had also destroyed the backbone of the RAF squadrons and seized all its northern airstrips.

It was a losing battle all the way and by 30 Jan 1942, the retreat of the British and Australians across the Causeway had begun. By

Left: The military band strikes up a tune to welcome fresh reinforcements from Britain.

Opposite below: An Indian Army gunner manning one of the massive 15-inch guns defending the southern shores of Singapore.

31 Jan, Johore was in the hands of the Japanese. The retreating forces blew up the Causeway behind them creating a 60-yard gap, but this was quickly repaired by Japanese engineers on 11 Feb.

One of the reasons for the swift descent of Japanese troops down Malaya was their ingenious use of bicycles and boats made of light steel and kapok wood, many of which were confiscated from the local population.

Lack of Northern Defences

Before the invasion, Lt. Gen. Percival, General Officer Commanding, Malaya, had ignored all proposals by his Chief Engineer, Brig. Ivan Simson to shore up the northern defences. Simson pointed out that all the fixed defences were guarding the south against an invasion from the sea. He was quite sure that the Japanese assault would come from the north, across the Straits instead.

However, Percival felt that it was bad for the morale of the troops and civilians if such measures were taken. Percival also believed that the Japanese assault, if it came from the north, would come from the northeast where four batteries of 6- and 15-inch guns provided firepower. An attack from the peninsula was unthinkable as it would get bogged down in the jungles. Thus, Singapore was deprived of solid northern defences.

Fortress Singapore

Till late 1941, everyone believed that Singapore, the "impregnable fortress", would not be affected by the war. She was protected from the north by the thick Malayan jungles and from the south by coastal guns, spotted all along the eastern and southwestern coasts of Singapore. Troop reinforcements and the arrival of the `Prince of Wales` and the `Repulse` lulled the people into feeling that the British could easily drive off the Japanese.

Singapore's Preparation for War

Percival had about 80,000 troops which were dispersed all over peninsular Malaya guarding airfields and important installations. He had no tanks (only light gun carriers) and 150 obsolete planes. His navy had suffered a great loss with the sinking of the `Prince of Wales` and the `Repulse`. Britain had no ships left to send down to Singapore, and the attack on the American Pacific Fleet meant that the U.S. had no battleships in the region that could assist the British.

The Japanese 25th Army — comprising the 5th, 18th and Imperial Guards Divisions — had about 67,000 men with 150 tanks and 560 aircraft. Though smaller in number in terms of troops, it had superior air support and tanks.

Besides the European troops, Singapore's local units consisted of four battalions of the Straits Settlements Volunteer Corps and a small civil defence force. With the impending Japanese threat, the Chinese put aside their various differences and offered their services to the governor, Sir Shenton Thomas. As a result, the Chinese National Council was formed on 31 Dec 1941 under the leadership of Tan Kah Kee, a prominent businessman.

Receiving enthusiastic Chinese support, the Council organised labour forces to maintain essential services and construct defence works. Selected members were trained for combat and guerilla warfare in Japanese-occupied territories. They soon became the pioneering members of the Malayan People's Anti-Japanese Army.

Australian troops taking up defensive positions in a series of withdrawals across the jungles of Malaya.

Percival's Defence Plans

Percival's plan for the defence of Singapore was to divide the country into three defence sectors. Lt. Gen. Sir Lewis Heath was put in command of the northern sector with the British 18th Division, the Indian 11th and 9th Divisions under his command; Maj. Gen. Gordon Bennett, commander of the Australian Imperial Forces, was in charge of the western sector with his fresh Australian troops and the untrained Indian 44th Infantry Brigade under his command; Maj. Gen. Keith Simmons took care of the southern sector, with the 1st and 2nd Malaya Infantry Regiment, the Straits Settlements Volunteer Force, fortress troops and fixed defences under his charge.

Bennett's 4.5-mile northwest coastline, stretching from Kranji River to Sarimbun River, was very weak. It was far too extended for his troops, numbering around 750 men. The mangrove swamps and heavy jungle prohibited construction of defence obstacles. This was to prove fatal later.

Yamashita's Assault Plans

At Kluang, Johore, on 1 Feb, Yamashita revealed his assault plans to his senior commanders. The initial thrust would be aimed at the northwestern shoreline. He tasked the 5th and 18th Divisions for the job. The Imperial Guards Division would create a diversion in the east (Pulau Ubin) to fool HQ Malaya Command, and heavy artillery bombardment would be directed along the entire northern sector of Singapore to conceal the actual landing areas.

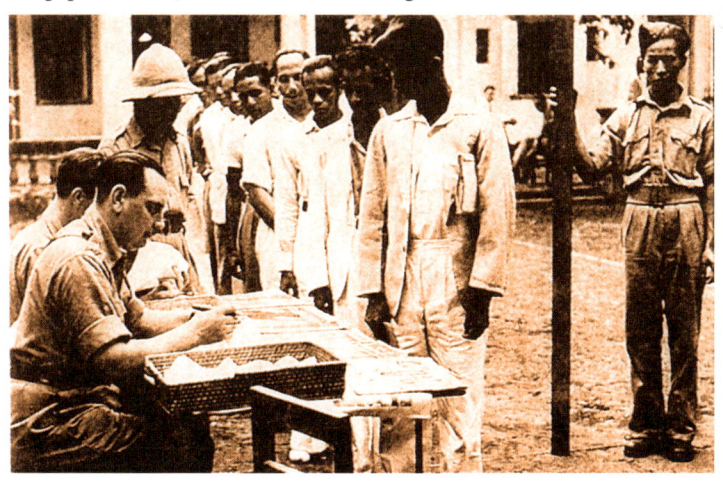

Local volunteers signing up for civil defence duties. The man on the right is holding a measuring stick to ensure that recruits meet the height requirement.

Lt. Gen. Arthur Ernest Percival, General Officer Commanding, HQ Malaya Command. He bore the brunt of the criticism when Malaya and Singapore surrendered in 70 days.

After securing a foothold in Singapore, Yamashita's first task was to capture Tengah airfield, followed by the capture of Mandai village. The next target was to be the Bukit Timah high ground, then to the Seletar, Peirce and MacRitchie reservoirs. Yamashita hoped to cut off the water supply to the island and force an early surrender of the British.

Meanwhile, the Japanese air force, superior over Singapore's air space, raided the Royal Navy's oil storage tanks at Sembawang Naval Base, sending huge columns of dense black smoke into the air. They also raided the Tanjong Pagar railway station.

Japanese intelligence despatched two teams of swimmers across the Straits on 3 Feb to gather information on the Australian artillery and troop positions. They reported back after three days with very accurate sketches.

On 6 Feb, Yamashita shifted his HQ to the Sultan of Johore's palace on Bukit Serene. This provided him with a good view of key targets, only a mile away across the Straits. The palace was never harassed by the British because it was the ancestral home of their old friend, Sultan Ibrahim. Any damage caused to his residence would have extensive repercussions to British-Johore ties.

Invasion of Singapore

Soon after nightfall on 7 Feb, 400 men of the Imperial Guards Division landed and took Pulau Ubin in a feint attack. They encountered minimum resistance. Though large troop movements in the rubber plantations across Johore had been sighted earlier, no action was taken as Percival received the news only hours before the attack.

The Japanese artillery began intensive firing the next day and Japanese pilots also began bombing military HQs within the western sector. Telegraph and telephone communications were destroyed in this bombardment. By nightfall, communications throughout the northwest defence areas were in shambles and communications between the frontline and command HQs were broken.

On the night of 8 Feb, Japanese troops of the 5th and 18th Division began to cross the water using sea craft hidden near the water's edge. These were launched in the backwaters of the Skudai, Danga, Perpet and Melayu rivers. This first assault was repelled by Australian machine-gunners, but other sea craft were able to seek and infiltrate gaps in the defence line.

By the third wave, the Australians were outnumbered and

overwhelmed as machine-gunners soon ran out of ammunition and the troops were crippled by the breakdown of communication with their command HQs.

At midnight, a red starshell burst over the Straits indicating to Yamashita the 5th Division's successful landing on Singapore soil. A white starshell burst later, to confirm the 18th Division's successful infiltration.

The Australian Forces were unable to hold back the Japanese advance towards Tengah airfield for long. The Australian commander, Brig. Taylor, planned to counterattack the Japanese's two-pronged movement towards Lim Chu Kang Rd and Choa Chu Kang Rd, but was foiled as his frontline troops were in disarray. He endeavoured to form a defence line, covering the northern approaches of Tengah airfield, running down Lim Chu Kang Rd to its junction with Choa Chu Kang Rd and westwards to Choa Chu Kang village. However, heavy artillery fire and Japanese air bombardment forced him to withdraw to the Kranji-Jurong Line in the afternoon of 9 Feb.

The Kranji-Jurong Line

The Kranji-Jurong Line is an arbitrary line running down from Kranji River to Jurong River. Loss of areas along this line meant that the Japanese would be able to advance down to the city from the west and through Bukit Timah Rd.

Due to the importance of this line, Percival ordered reinforce-

Above: Lt. Gen. Tomoyuki Yamashita, also known as the "Tiger of Malaya", led the conquering Japanese forces.

Below: Singapore city after a bombing attack. For many civilians, the wailing sound of sirens signalled death and destruction.

15

Above: *Even the Victoria Memorial Hall was not spared the ravages of the Japanese bombing.*

Opposite: *A local farmer contemplates his uncertain future as oil tanks set alight by retreating British forces burn in the background.*

ments to the Bukit Panjang-Keat Hong Rd junction to the right of the Line. One Australian brigade was to remain holding the Causeway sector while another brigade would try to stabilise the Kranji-Jurong Line. The Indian 44th Brigade in the west was also withdrawn to the left of the Kranji-Jurong Line while another Indian brigade was to move to the Bukit Timah racecourse to protect the island's vital food and petrol dumps located near by.

Percival's Last-Ditch Plans

However, Percival knew that this might not be enough to hold back the Japanese and he made preparations for a last desperate stand. He planned to hold a perimeter covering Kallang airfield, MacRitchie and Peirce reservoirs and the Bukit Timah supply depot area. He issued this instruction in secret to his three generals. But these instructions were soon to be misunderstood by Brig. Taylor.

The Japanese at Kranji

On 10 Feb, the Japanese suffered one of their major losses at the Kranji River. The Imperial Guards had begun their assault on the night of the 9th and while moving up the Kranji River, got bogged down in the mangrove swamps and lost in its tributaries. Shortly after midnight, many died when they were burned by the flaming oil from demolished fuel tanks which gushed into the water.

Gen. Nishimura, the Commanding General of the Imperial Guards, wanted to withdraw in panic, but was reprimanded by Yamashita. However, through a misunderstanding of orders, the defending Australians started withdrawing from the Causeway sector, giving the invaders the liberty to move further inland.

It was also at this time that Yamashita first stepped onto Singapore in the predawn darkness. He set up his HQ in a rubber plantation just north of Tengah airfield.

Loss of the Kranji-Jurong Line

Over at the Kranji-Jurong Line, Brig. Taylor who received a message adapted by Bennett regarding Percival's last-ditch plans misread them. He took it as an instruction to proceed immediately to the defence perimeter positions. This set into motion a series of related withdrawals from the northern sector of the Kranji-Jurong Line which allowed the Japanese to swiftly take control of Woodlands Rd.

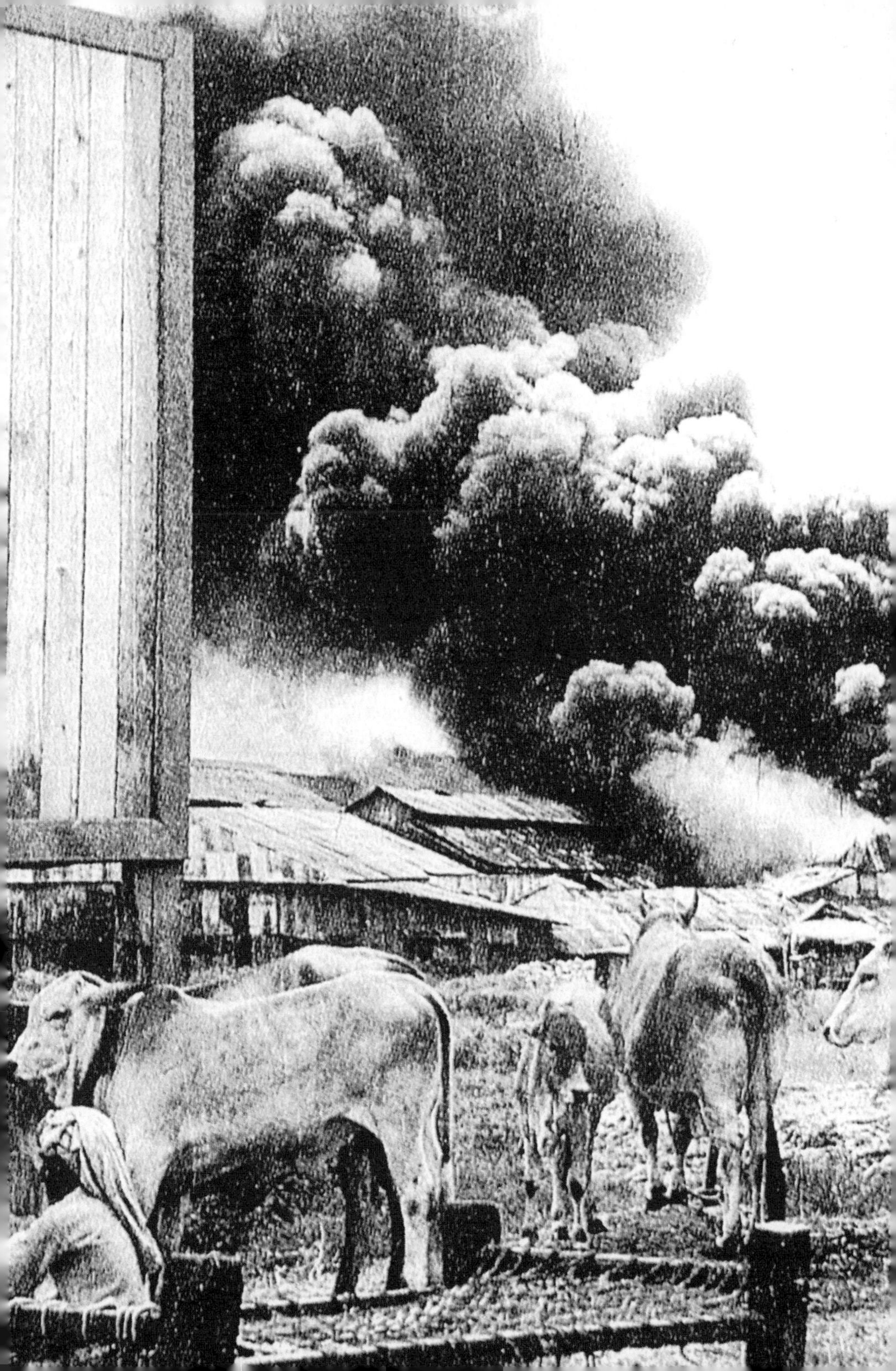

Fortress Singapore

At 1.30 pm on the same day, the Indian 44th Brigade was also in full retreat from the southern extreme of the Kranji-Jurong Line following clashes with Japanese Infantry units and having suffered heavy air and artillery bombardments. Through a series of miscalculations and miscommunications, the Kranji-Jurong Line was wrested away from the British by mid-afternoon.

Japanese tanks also made their first appearance on the island on 10 Feb. They were floated across the Straits to Lim Chu Kang Rd early in the day, and joined in the battle at dusk. They made their way down Choa Chu Kang Rd and stopped at the Bukit Panjang village and Bukit Timah Rd junction to wait for ammunition supplies and support artillery. The Australian troops were no match for the tanks and fled to the hills east of Bukit Panjang village.

Further Retreat of the Defenders

11 Feb was Kigensetsu, the anniversary celebration of the coronation of Emperor Jimmu, the day Yamashita had hoped to capture Singapore. Ammunition supplies were running low for the Japanese forces. He had letters dropped over HQ Malaya Command areas urging Percival to give up his desperate fight, thus hoping for an early surrender.

Japanese troops made rapid advance thanks to the roads built by the British and bicycles stolen from the local population.

The Malayan Campaign

In their retreat, the British destroyed bridges to slow down the Japanese juggernaut. This failed to dent the advance as the Imperial army crossed rivers in canoes to continue harassing the disorganised British troops.

With the collapse of the Kranji-Jurong Line, the Imperial Guards started to move down to their target, the MacRitchie and Peirce reservoirs. They had also managed to repair the Causeway and began moving more men and equipment across.

With the rapid Japanese approach, Percival moved his HQ from Sime Rd to the underground Fort Canning Bunker. This was his last HQ in Singapore and it was here that he made the decision to surrender four days later.

The defending troops, by this time, were badly shaken. Thousands of exhausted and frightened stragglers left the fighting to seek shelter in large commercial buildings.

On 12 Feb, the defenders clashed with Japanese troops at Bukit Timah Rd, south of Bukit Timah village, Nee Soon village and Pasir Panjang.

Over at the Fort Canning Bunker, also known as "The Battlebox", Percival marked out Singapore's final protective perimeter. It was 28 miles long enclosing Kallang airfield, Thomson village, MacRitchie Reservoir, and Adam, Farrer, Holland and Buona Vista roads.

Yamashita moved his HQ forward to the bomb-damaged Ford Motor Factory on 13 Feb. He feared a prolonged war once Percival had dug in at his last defensive position to wait for relief reinforcements. He had not enough men or the ammunition for a long war.

Above: Japanese infantrymen attacking British positions along the Bukit Timah area.

Below: Many skirmishes took place in the towns.

Fortress Singapore

Thus, he tasked the 18th Division to capture Alexandra Barracks and the Imperial Guards to capture MacRitchie quickly before Percival had settled in at his last stand.

Pasir Panjang Battle

It was at Pasir Panjang Ridge that the 1st and 3rd Battalion Malay Regiment began their epic 48-hour stand against the Japanese. They held on stubbornly while others along the lines were toppling. Only when the regiments were almost wiped out to a man was the ridge given up.

Over at the Fort Canning Battlebox, Heath and Bennett urged Percival to surrender as the civilian toll was mounting while the troops were too exhausted, demoralised and disorganised to continue. Percival, however, still refused to do so.

14 Feb dawned bitterly on the defending forces. The 18th Division continued their assault on the hapless Malay Regiment and the Imperial Guards swarmed out of the MacRitchie area to battle the British. Water failure was imminent and an epidemic threatened the overpopulated city.

The Japanese also extracted their revenge for the bitter battle at Pasir Panjang by storming Alexandra Hospital and bayoneting staff and patients alike. About 200 innocent victims were murdered.

During the last days of the Malayan Campaign, the population was thrown into absolute panic. In the chaos and pandemonium, many families were separated. The women and children tried to escape to India or Australia. Tragically, many never reached their destinations as Japanese planes torpedoed their ships.

Defeat

On Sunday 15 Feb, Japanese troops broke through the north of the city as the defending troops along the south coast were retreating. Food stocks were not expected to last another two days and ammunition stocks for the defenders within their lines would last only for a few more hours. The available fuel was only what was in the tanks of the vehicles. The water supply was on the point of collapse. In the morning conference with his field commanders, Percival proposed two solutions: a counterattack to wrest back MacRitchie Reservoir to restore the water supply and retake food depots or a decision to surrender. All his commanders opted for surrender.

A three-man deputation was sent to Bukit Timah Rd at 2 pm. Negotiations with Lt. Col. Sugita of the Japanese Army took place. Instructed to raise a Japanese flag above the Cathay building, the deputation then left after agreeing to a meeting later that day at about 4 pm. After the deputation had returned to Fort Canning, Percival and the deputation made their way to Bukit Timah Rd, to be met by Lt. Col. Sugita and brought to the Ford Motor Factory at about 5.15 pm. It was here that Percival met Yamashita for the first time. Percival tried to stall for time, but Yamashita demanded an immediate unconditional surrender or a massive assault on the city would follow. Percival gave in and signed the surrender document at about 6.10 pm.

21

Above: Percival (extreme right) marches along with his delegation and Lt. Col. Sugita to his fateful meeting with Yamashita. Percival's plans were to negotiate for time from the Japanese to reorganise his troops and wait for reinforcements.

Opposite: In the face of defeat, British troops set fire to oil tanks in a "scorched earth" policy to prevent them from falling into Japanese hands.

The Japanese had defeated the British in only 10 weeks. The main reason for the British defeat was that Britain was also tied up with the war in Europe and North Africa. She was fighting against Germany and Italy and could not afford to spread her resources to the Far East.

The British also underestimated the Japanese and were unprepared for the enemy's war hardiness. Whitehall thought that the Japanese air force would not be superior to theirs so they only had 158 ageing "Brewster Buffalos" in Malaya against the hundreds of advanced "Zero" fighters.

Thinking that tanks were not suitable for jungle warfare, the British leaders in London did not supply them to Malaya while the Japanese came armed with 150 light tanks. The British also did not have enough anti-tank guns to counter the Japanese tank attack which was thought inconceivable.

Finally, the ill-trained soldiers of the British and Allied forces contributed to the rapid fall. The Japanese soldiers were not only well trained in jungle warfare, but also had war experience after fighting on the China front. The British troops, on the other hand, were mostly young men conscripted into a war for which many of them were never properly trained. This, together with the lack of logistic support and the physically tiring travels on board ships over long distances, took their toll on the soldiers.

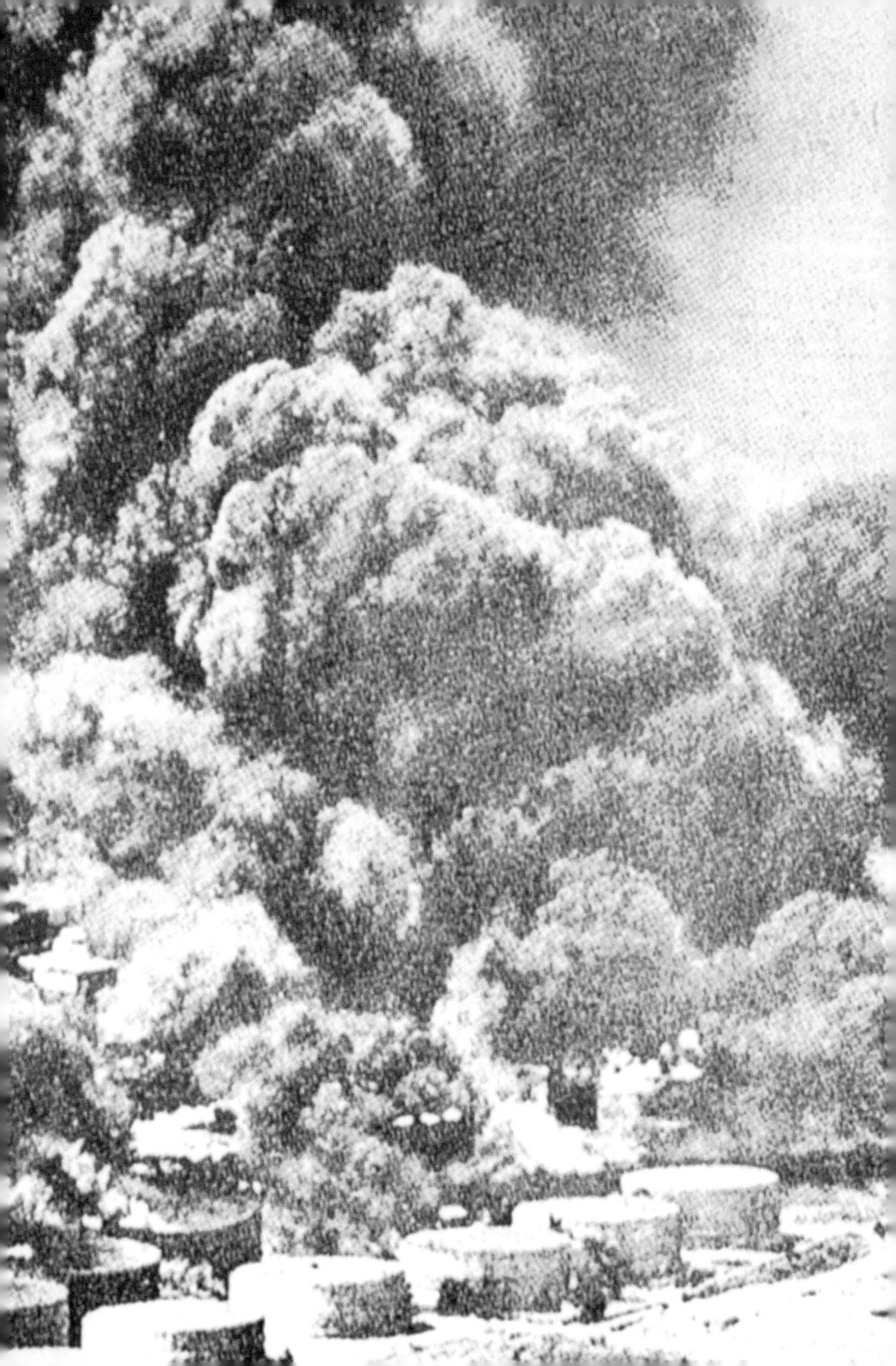

The Japanese Occupation

When the curtain fell on the opening act of the war, one million inhabitants were condemned to play out the scenes of life under Japanese Occupation. The scenes were of an all-too-grim reality. Chaos, panic and looting marked the first days after the surrender. Homes were stripped of all valuables that could be sold on the black market. Both soldiers and civilians were active participants. The European residential district of Holland Rd, Tanglin Rd and Bukit Timah were the favourite looting spots. The people used vans, lorries or went on foot to carry away their spoils. Eight looters were foolhardy enough to break into a Japanese military store and kill the sentry. They were hunted, caught and beheaded. Their heads were put on spikes and displayed at Tanjong Pagar, Stamford Rd, Fullerton Square, Dhoby Ghaut and Kallang Bridge. The severity of the punishment was effective — looting stopped.

The streets of the city were dirty, smelly and devastated. Shops were closed, and dead bodies lay in the streets and damaged buildings. The stench of the decomposing bodies filled the air while people searched for their loved ones among the rubble. Some survived, others were not so fortunate.

The frustration of fighting 70 days down the entire length of the Malayan peninsula must have taken its toll on Japanese self-control, for especially in the first days of occupation, the soldiers ill-treated the population. In Havelock Rd, when a couple was "rude" enough not to get down from their rickshaw and pay respects while passing by, the soldiers demanded that the husband run and pull the rickshaw instead, while forcing the coolie to sit beside the wife.

Soldiers slapped and kicked people at will, and made some kneel on the roadside for hours. People who did not give respectful bows to sentries were tied to lampposts for the entire day. The soldiers would return in the evening to untie the person who, by that time, was dehydrated, sunburnt and very ill.

Sook Ching Operation

The Japanese had been at war with China since 1937. The years of difficult, costly and brutal warfare had engendered in the Japanese a hatred of the Chinese.

Overseas Chinese in Singapore had supported the war effort in China by supplying men, equipment and money. Overseas Chinese also fought as members of the Straits Settlements Volunteer Force against the Japanese invasion of Singapore. Thus, they had to be eliminated.

The Japanese Occupation

A startling decree was issued to the population: All males in Syonan-To between the ages of 18 and 50 years were to report to five registration centres at noon on 21 Feb, 1942. This was just seven days after the surrender. The question on everyone's lips was: "Why?"

Maj. Gen. Kawamura, commander of the Singapore garrison, went to 25th Army Headquarters to question the wisdom of the order. He was told that Lt. Gen. Yamashita had personally approved it. There was nothing he could do.

Meanwhile, the Kempeitai, the Japanese military police, were dragging people out of their homes at bayonet point. The men who voluntarily went to the registration centres thought they were going to get jobs. Jalan Besar, Arab St, Tanjong Pagar, the junction of Kallang and Geylang Rd, the junction of River Valley and Clemenceau Ave and Paya Lebar rubber estate were the main areas. At these centres, the men were separated into groups: civil servants, students, hawkers and merchants. The centres had no toilets, food or shade. In Geylang, the people were made to stay in the open field under the tropical sun for the whole day. A minor reporting centre was located at the corner of Upper Cross St and South Bridge Rd. The ends of the streets were cordoned off to serve as a pen.

The men were questioned about their jobs, asked to write their names and checked for tattoo marks. English-speaking Chinese were considered dangerous; tattoo marks meant one was a secret

Above: Little Tokyo: a scene in downtown Singapore during the Occupation. Singapore was renamed Syonan-To, meaning "Light of the South."

Below: Just after the war, Japanese soldiers executed locals who were suspected of being loyal to the British. It is estimated that between 25,000 and 50,000 people were murdered.

25

Above: Allied POWs were reduced to skin and bones on a meagre diet of rice gruel alone.

Below: After shooting their victims, Japanese soldiers bayoneted them to make sure that no one would live to tell the tale. Surprisingly, a few men managed to feign death and survived this traumatic event.

society member. Those who could not write their names in Chinese were ridiculed and in danger of being shot. The original idea of the Sook Ching operation was to weed out anti-Japanese elements, but the order was carried out by subordinates who were indiscriminate. Those who "failed" the questioning were taken away in truckloads to the beaches of Punggol and Changi to be shot. Those who satisfied the interrogators were given a chop with the Japanese word "examined" on their arms or clothes. It was not an absolute guarantee of safety, for some unfortunate ones were rearrested and shot.

In those terrible days, one person was the saviour of many a Chinese man. His name was Mamoru Shinozaki. A humane civilian administrator, he used his position to set up the Overseas Chinese Association for the protection of the Chinese. He meant for the association to act as a cover for the Chinese. He used his influence with the Kempeitai to take people out of the Kempeitai prisons and registration centres, saving more than 2,000 people during the Sook Ching operation. Some of the men had protection cards signed by Mr Shinozaki smuggled in to them.

Mr Chan Cheng Yean was a Singapore Volunteer soldier. His unit was captured, separated by race, and marched from Race Course Rd to Tanjong Katong Rd. They were placed under the sun in an open field until three or four lorries came and took them to Bedok. There were 90 of them divided into groups of three men, all

The Japanese Occupation

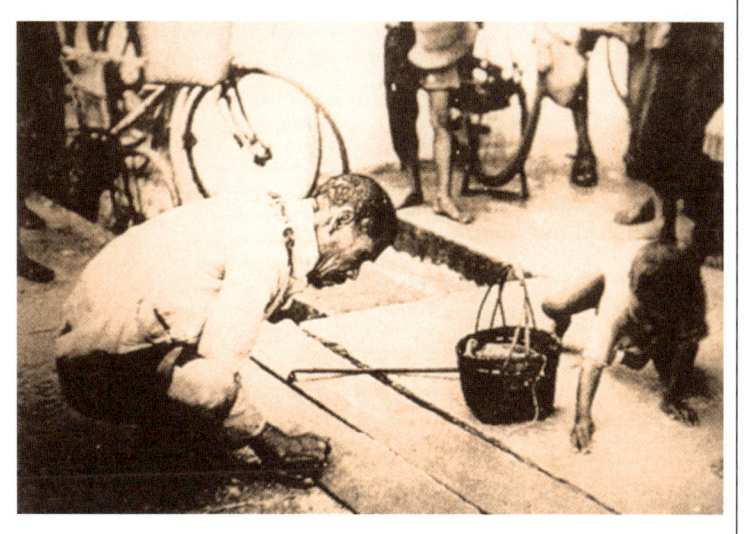

standing in front of an open trench. They stood close to each other until there was no room to move. Then they were shot, group by group. Mr Chan, who stood with the second group, was shot in the knee, and fell into the trench with the dead. "They went down like toy soldiers," he recounted.

He held his breath while the Japanese soldiers came around to check and bayonet the bodies. The incident took 20 minutes. He heard footsteps moving away and waited another 15 minutes before he tried getting out. He pushed against the planks that were placed on top of them and untangled his legs from the bodies to crawl out. He was the only one alive.

The military authorities finally saw the futility of the operation. They were making enemies of the Chinese in Singapore and that would make administration difficult. But by then the damage was done. The official estimate was 6,000 dead. Local estimates had it anywhere from 25,000 to 50,000 dead.

Much anguish, pain and suffering resulted from the conduct of the Kempeitai, who conducted counter-espionage activities. Their methods of torture gained them infamy and the unequivocal hatred of both locals and foreigners. Persons caught listening to illegal radios had pencils put into their ears which were then forced inwards. The "water treatment" had victims pumped full with water and the soldiers would then jump repeatedly on their water-filled bellies. These Kempeitai soldiers with their distinct armbands struck

Above: Food was so scarce during the Occupation that even the grains of rice that had fallen to the floor were carefully scooped up and eaten. Besides rice, tapioca and sweet potatoes were staple diet and, often, the only sources of food.

Below: Ration cards were issued in an attempt to ease the food shortages. Many people resorted to eating snakes, rodents, dogs and other animals.

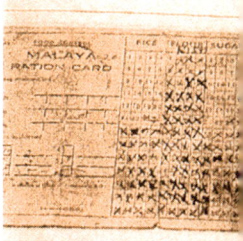

terror wherever they went. The name Kempeitai became synonymous with cruelty, terror and death. Mr Rob Scott, a man who survived the tortures, described the Kempeitai soldiers as "spoilt boys of fourteen, headstrong, selfish, brutal." He added, "... like children, they are insensitive to criticism."

$50 Million Gift

The Chinese population had hardly recovered from the Sook Ching operation when another shock hit them. The Occupation masters decreed that the Chinese in Malaya had to "donate" $50 million in gratitude for the sparing of their lives and property. In actual fact, the Japanese needed the money to sustain their army and supplies. Extortion of the Chinese was one of the means, hence the "donation".

The Chinese in Singapore had to come up with $10 million. Through a series of levies, the amount collected was only $25 million, the balance of which was made up by a loan from a Japanese bank. $15 million was deposited with the Japanese Treasury while the rest was ostensibly for the setting up of a bank, relief work, road and bridge reconstruction, the setting up of a training institute for youths, and the creation of an endowment fund for the issue of Reconstruction bonds. However, the bank was never set up, roads and bridges were instead stripped of metal; the institute was for espionage training and the bonds were exploitative.

The price of foodstuffs skyrocketed and the Japanese "banana money" were made worthless as black markets began appearing overnight.

		1941 $	1945 $
RICE	1 picul	5.00	5,000.00
EGG	1 dozen	0.24	120.00
PARKER PEN	1	15.00	5,000.00
QUININE POWDER	1 lb	1.50	15.00
BERIN VITAMIN B1	500 pills	26.00	45,000.00
SHOPHOUSE	1	5,000–6,000	160,000–250,000

Shortages, Rationing and Substitutes

On 5 June, 1942, in the Battle of Midway, the Japanese Imperial Navy lost four aircraft carriers and their complement of crew and planes. It was the turning point of the war. The Japanese were thrown on the defensive. Japanese ship transports increasingly became the target of Allied submarines. Shopkeepers withheld goods because it was more profitable to sell on the black market.

A rationing system was implemented and 2- to 3-hour line-ups once a month for basic foodstuffs became a normal occurrence. The quality of food was nothing to rave about: "... we remember the bread we got. It was like rubber. When you throw it, it can bounce." The ration of eight catties of rice per month was cut to six. Most of the food had to come overland from Thailand. Singapore was turned into a big garden city under the Grow More Food policy introduced by the Japanese military administration, the Tokubetsu. Every available plot of land was used to cultivate food. And food was not getting any cheaper. In the black market, a dozen eggs fetched a price of $120 by 1944. A case of powdered milk, a much sought-after product, cost $25,000. A tin of butter would fetch $950 and a tin of State Express cigarettes $5,000. People patched and repatched their clothes because a yard of cloth cost $300 to $400. The Tokubetsu tried to control the situation, but they found themselves having to go into the black market to get what they needed.

Tapioca became the main staple because it was easier to cultivate. A whole range of substitutes sprang up as the people stretched their ingenuity, imagination and resources to feed, clothe and wash themselves. Cakes, bread and cookies were made with sago flour. The Japanese authorities said: "Though these [substitutes] differ from those made with wheat flour, they have tastes of their own." Condensed milk was made by adding sugar to fresh milk and boiling it for hours. People also made their own soap.

Education

The Japanese language was taught in schools and adults were encouraged to learn Japanese in night schools. It was hoped that this would lead to an appreciation of the superior culture of the Japanese. Besides, it would also make administration and control of the population easier.

The older students were more anxious about the number of years they would miss in school and when the British came back, some of

Japanese was made the official language and everyone had to learn and converse in it.

The Shonan Times was the official mouthpiece of the Japanese propaganda machine. Many people risked their lives to operate a radio and listen to news of the war on the BBC.

them found themselves in a class three or four years higher, and they could not cope. "Some of them could not read the books they were given," recalled Mr Gay, a teacher during the Occupation. Because of the emphasis on learning Japanese, no English lessons were given although the teachers had to teach in English because they were not proficient in Japanese

Endau Settlement

By mid-1943, the Japanese position in the Pacific was deteriorating. They lost Attu in the Aleutian islands, which cut the Japanese defence chain across the Pacific. The Americans, by sheer numbers, overwhelmed them on the Solomon and Gilbert islands.

Because of this series of events, the food situation got worse in Singapore. The Grow More Food campaign became urgent. There were simply not enough supplies getting through the Allied blockade of the shipping lanes. There was not enough land to grow food to feed the one million inhabitants. Where were the authorities going to find enough food? The 7th Area Army, under Itagaki Seishino, was in charge of the administration of Malaya and passed down an order to the Tokubetsu.

This order from the 7th Area Army headquarters held the rank of a battle operation order "C-No. 1." It was the strongest order issued to the Tokubetsu during the war. It read thus:

"The Syonan Tokubetsu must execute this evacuation order immediately. The Military Administration Headquarters will assist the Tokubetsu where necessary to implement it. The evacuation target is 300,000. Tokubetsu shall select a suitable site to receive the people from Syonan. The necessary materials and transport will be provided by the Army."

Mayor Naito Kanichi appointed Mr Shinozaki to implement the order. Mr Shinozaki enlisted the help of the Overseas Chinese Association and got approval for his proposal that the settlement be self-governing and out of the jurisdiction of the Kempeitai and the police. The Association supported the idea, set up a working committee and got things under way. A site was chosen in southeastern Johore, called Endau. The site was cleared of jungle and wild animals, a road was built into the settlement, and land cultivated to grow rice and vegetables.

In September 1943, ten lorry-loads of people from Singapore were the first joyful settlers of Endau, or New Syonan. The settlement grew

The Japanese Occupation

larger by the day. Restaurants and schools were set up, a branch of the Overseas-Chinese Banking Corporation was opened; streets were named after the officials, and shops sold vegetables grown by the settlers. A delicacy of the settlement was lizard meat soup.

There were temporary tensions when Chinese guerillas of the Malayan People's Anti-Japanese Army raided the settlement to steal rice, but they were appeased and peace returned to the settlement. By the end of the first year, 12,000 people lived in New Syonan.

Another settlement was also set up in Bahau, Negri Sembilan. It was called Fuji Village, and this settlement was populated mainly by Eurasians. However, poor land and disease doomed the project.

Life for the POWs in Changi worsened as the war dragged on. Lack of food, water and proper medicine took their toll on many men.

Allied Victory

By September 1944, the Japanese had lost air bases in Rabaul, the Marianas and Caroline islands and the northern coast of New Guinea. The battle for the Philippines had begun. People heard of the Japanese reversals in the Pacific on their illegal radios and rejoiced inwardly. The value of the Japanese military currency — known as "banana money" — plunged daily and prices rocketed.

When the Philippines was lost to the Allies in January 1945, the war moved to the doorstep of Japan. Cities in Japan were bombed, the sea lanes cut off and vital oil supplies to Japan dried up. In Europe, Germany had surrendered in May 1945, and now the Russians were looming over Japan.

American B-29 Superfortresses started appearing over Singapore and bombed Seletar Naval Base, the harbour and the city. Life was as difficult as ever, but the people could sense the end was near. The Japanese made preparations for the expected assault on Singapore — forced labour was employed to dig defences. Japanese women were given training in weapons handling, civilians were either evacuated or mobilised as civil defence personnel.

By then, Operation Zipper, the Allies' massive assault to retake Malaya and Singapore, had already been set in motion. An overwhelming force of aircraft carriers, battle cruisers and destroyers, carrying ground forces and Spitfire aircraft, was on its way to the peninsula.

The assault, however, never took place. On the morning of 6 August 1945, an American B-29 bomber dropped an atomic bomb on the city of Hiroshima. Then, on 9 August, Russia declared war on Japan, destroying their only hope of mediation and, shortly after, the second atomic bomb fell on Nagasaki. The two bombs killed a total of 101,903 people and injured 94,068.

Faced with the devastation, declining war efforts and a torn Cabinet, Emperor Hirohito officially issued the order to surrender

Above: Streets packed with people ready to welcome back the British Commonwealth troops.

Opposite Below: Victory parades marked the return of the British.

on 15 August 1945. All over Singapore, Allied bombers dropped leaflets onto the streets to inform the people that the war was indeed over.

The first Allied troops were, however, not to set foot on Singapore until two weeks after the surrender. During that period of general lawlessness and uncertainty, looting was commonplace. Bitter people took revenge on locals who had collaborated with the Japanese during the Occupation period and mistreated them. Force 136 guerrillas set up headquarters in a hotel at Rangoon Road and began a systematic house-to-house search for collaborators, shooting and torturing any they found.

The Japanese troops in Singapore remained unhappy about their orders to surrender. Many would rather have fought to the end. Scores of Japanese soldiers committed *hara-kiri* — honourable suicide by disembowelment. Others held drinking parties in their houses before blowing themselves up with dynamite.

Lt. Gen. Itagaki signing the Surrender Document at City Hall on 12 September 1945.

On 5 September 1945, the British 5th Indian Division arrived at Tanjong Pagar Docks, watched by a cheering crowd. Athough the disembarkment was slowed down by the dilapidated state of the docks, over the next few days, Allied forces swiftly reoccupied the entire island, taking control of military installations, gathering the Japanese in concentration areas and restoring order. The British Military Administration was established to resolve the problems of food shortage, rampant inflation and unemployment.

The buoyant mood of the people climaxed on 12 September 1945 when, at the Municipal Buildings, Lord Admiral Mountbatten, Supreme Commander of the Allied Forces, accepted the surrender of all Japanese forces in Southeast Asia. The Union Jack was hoisted to the anthems of the Allied nations, and for hundreds of locals, internees and prisoners of war in the euphoric crowd, the nightmare years were finally over.

Lord Louis Mountbatten leaving City Hall after accepting the Japanese surrender. The war had finally come to an end.

The Causeway linking Singapore to Malaya was blown up, creating a 60-yard gap in the middle. In the centre of the picture stands the palace of the Sultan of Johore that was used as a command post by Lt. Gen. Yamashita.

THE NORTHWESTERN TOUR

Kranji Reservoir Park

Facing Johore, this northwestern stretch of Singapore was where the Japanese troops first landed. The Japanese fooled the British into thinking that they would attack from the northeast by invading Pulau Ubin. The day after the attack, the 5th and 18th Division of the Japanese forces landed on the northwestern coast of Singapore, from Kranji, Lim Chu Kang down to Sarimbun. These areas were defended by the 22nd Brigade of the Australian Imperial Forces and by the Singapore Chinese Anti-Japanese Volunteer Battalion. These Chinese volunteers were collectively named the Dalforce, after their commander, Lt. Col. John Dalley.

The Dalforce consisted of mainly Chinese prisoners who had been serving sentences in Changi Prison. They were largely untrained, receiving only a 10-day crash course and equipped with uniforms and elementary weapons. They suffered heavy casualties in the fighting and as a result of their involvement in the war, suffered bitter reprisals by the Japanese.

The Japanese were able to gain a footing on the northwestern shores because the Australians were too thinly spread out: 750 men stretched over a 4.5 mile segment of the frontline from Kranji River westwards to Sarimbun River. Artillery support was also slow in coming due to a breakdown in communication lines, Thus, the defending troops were left totally without support. As Singapore is a small island, movement of troops and support could have been done much faster.

It was not as if no attempt was made to determine the actual direction of attack by the Japanese. As late as 7 Feb 1942, two Australian patrols were sent across to Johore but were still unable to detect Japanese forces. They saw large enemy reinforcements arriving in the rubber plantations opposite the western shores of the island between the Skudai and Perpet rivers. But this information was only passed on to the HQ Malaya Command in the afternoon the next day, less than six hours before the Japanese attacked. As the patrols failed to locate any boats (these were hidden further in), Percival thought it was unlikely that the Japanese would attack so soon. The earliest date expected of the attack was on the 10th or 11th of Feb though the Japanese had been firing heavily at the defenders on the western

Above: Japanese troops cross the Causeway after repairing the 60-yard gap created by retreating British forces.

Opposite Below: The invasion of Singapore began on the night of 8 Feb 1942, when soldiers from the 5th and 18th Divisions landed on the northwestern coast of Singapore.

Fortress Singapore

side throughout the morning of 8 Feb, cutting and disrupting road movement.

The Japanese infiltrated steadily in widely scattered defensive positions on the northwest and made for the neck of land between Ama Keng on the Kranji River and Sungei Berih. Their plan was to get hold of Tengah airfield and to gain control of Bukit Timah Rd which leads to the heart of the island. The Australians were forced to retreat and the Japanese soon occupied Ama Keng village, close to the Kranji River.

The British had no choice but to fall back on their next line of defence which was to be the Kranji-Jurong Line. This was the ground between Kranji River in the north and Jurong River in the south, through which two major roads ran, Choa Chu Kang Rd and Jurong Rd. Here, units of the Australian forces, the 12th, 15th and 44th Brigade of the Indian Forces, and the Special Reserve Battalion were to face the Japanese 5th and 8th Divisions. (The 5th Division was commanded by Lt. Gen. Takuro Matsui and the 18th Division by Lt. Gen. Renya Mutaguchi.)

The mouth of the Kranji River today. This was the scene of confused and distraught fighting as the Australian soldiers tried desperately to defend against the overwhelming enemy advance.

N1 Kranji Reservoir Park

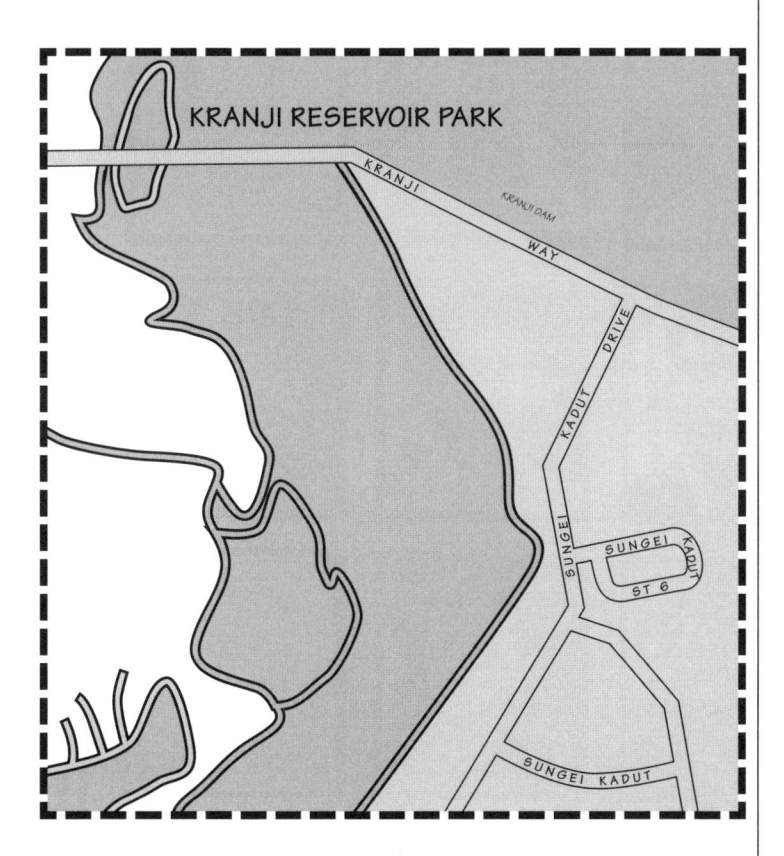

Notes

The Kranji site is easily accessible by car. The mouth of the Kranji River has been dammed, but one can see the thrust of the Japanese invasion when standing in the park.

Fortress Singapore

Sarimbun Beach Battle Site

Surprise Attack!!

The British surmised that any attack by the Japanese army would be by sea. General Percival himself judged that the Japanese would attack on the northeast sector and prepared to defend it aggressively. As it turned out, the Japanese had other plans. General Yamashita devised a tactical cover and deception plan to launch a feint landing on Pulau Ubin and then spring a surprise attack on the 8-km wide coastline near Sarimbun. The aim was to achieve a surprise break-in, establish an initial bridgehead line-up to Tengah Airbase and subsequently capture the Sungei Jurong and Bukit Mandai line. All forces were then to reconstitute along that line in preparation for the city attack.

On 8 Feb 1942, the Japanese artillery east of Johore Bahru

The Northwestern Tour

Left: Sarimbun Beach Battle Site.

Opposite Below: View from the Sarimbun Beach Battle Site.

Page 44: The National Heritage Board's historic marker for the Sarimbun Beach landing site.

continuously fired towards Changi. As planned, this successfully diverted British attention to northeast Singapore so that their intended target, the northwest would be weakly defended when Japanese troops eventually landed. The guns were scattered about in ones and twos to give the impression that each gun position might be a battery. This led the British to estimate that there were no less than six Japanese artillery regiments present. So successful was Japanese deception that British artillery in north Singapore engaged in fierce counter-battery work.

Meanwhile, the true location of the impending Japanese assault, the northwest corner of Singapore, remained weakly defended. Throughout the day, the Japanese fired heavy barrages. Starting at about 10.00 am, they pounded the area around Bukit Mandai, Seletar Pier, Sembawang Airbase and Tengah Airbase with some 25,000 rounds of ammunition. Following this, they fired onto key strongholds along the coast. The artillery barrages were intensified as the Japanese army prepared to land at Sarimbun. A little past midnight, the red and green flares were sighted confirming the successful landing of the Japanese 5th and 18th Division Artillery Regiments.

In the battle that ensued at Sarimbun, the British were ill-equipped to deal with the assault force. The defended posts were widely separated and there were insufficient local reserves available for immediate counter-attack. The 22nd Australian Brigade entrusted with the defence of the front where the landing took place was given an impossible task. By 9 Feb, the Japanese had overrun this brigade and made their way to Tengah airfield.

SARIMBUN BEACH
LANDING

N2 Sarimbun Beach Battle Site

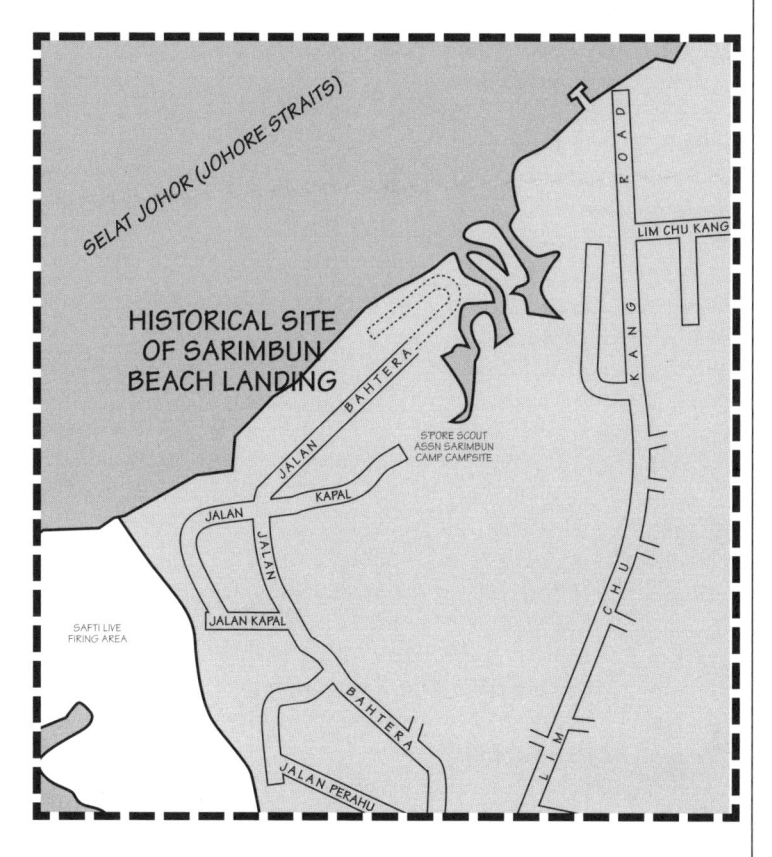

Notes

Protected by heavy artillery fire, Japanese soldiers from the 5th and 18th Division crossed the Johore Straits in a fleet of small boats and landed at Sarimbun on the night of 8 Feb 1942. The Sarimbun Beach Battle Site is located on Jalan Bahtera.

Kranji War Memorial

After the British surrendered on 15 Feb, 1942, a prisoner-of-war camp and hospital was set up at the present location of the Kranji War Memorial. Prior to this, a military camp and ammunition magazine was located on the same site. The cemetery was started by the hospital inmates during the Occupation, serving as a resting place for British servicemen who died in prison.

When the war ended, this military cemetery was expanded by the Army War Graves Service to include other British military burials from all parts of the island. The present form was arranged by the Commonwealth War Graves Commission. The large oval-shaped memorial (the 12-panelled structure at the far end), with its aerofoil layout, dominates the skyline. On its 12 panels are recorded the names of 23,943 men and women who have no known graves.

Around it are memorials to other British military casualties of the Malayan Campaign buried all over Southeast Asia. These include those who died and were buried in the grounds of the General Hospital as well as Chinese members of the Commonwealth forces massacred during the Occupation and troops buried in Indo-China (Vietnam) and Burma (Myanmar). There is also an Indian Memorial to commemorate those accorded the last cremation rites. There are 4,464 individual burials marked by headstones laid out in neat rows on this

The Northwestern Tour

smooth lawn. Flowering shrubs and trees were added to make this a lovely and peaceful place for families of those buried here to pay their respects.

The names of all the British military personnel buried here are recorded in a memorial book kept by the custodian who lives just next to the memorial. The names of Australians, Britons, Malays, Indians and Chinese can be found at the memorial. The youngest was no more than 16 years of age. Every year on 11 Nov, a commemorative service is held to honour these brave defenders. These services are usually attended by representatives from countries who have their war dead here (namely from Britain, New Zealand, Australia and Malaysia).

The soldiers are honoured in the Far East Prisoner Of War Prayer recited at each commemorative service.

Above: A monument to those whose remains were never found.

Below: The steeple with a cross greets the visitor from afar.

Opposite Below: Names of men from the Commonwealth forces are found on inscribed tombstones. Many were young and able men in their 20's.

47

And we that are left
Grow old with the years
Remembering the heartache,
The pain and the tears;
Hoping and praying
That never again man will sink
To such sorrow and shame
The price that was paid
We will always remember
Every day, every month
Not just in November.

N3 **Kranji War Memorial**

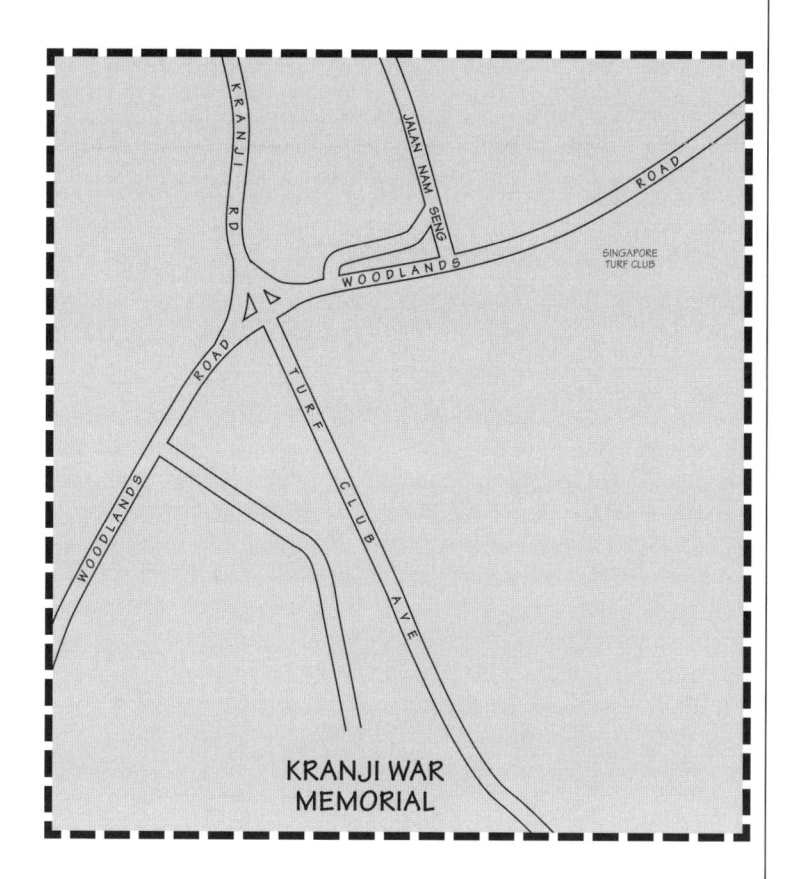

Notes

Kranji War Memorial is located close to the reservoir park. There is no charge for entry and from this hill one can see for miles on a clear day.

Bukit Batok Hilltop

One of the fiercest battles was fought in the Bukit Batok area. As a result, in June 1942, the Japanese wanted to build a war memorial and Shinto temple here using British and Australian prisoners-of-war from Sime Rd Camp. This was also to honour their comrades who had died in the campaign. The memorial site chosen was near the then Ford Motor Factory. A group of POWs was put to work on the monument, assisting the Japanese engineering corps under the supervision of Lt. Toshiyuki Nekemoto.

As a result of building the monuments, the POWs wanted to organise search parties of their own to gather their unburied dead left in the jungles. The Japanese engineering commander-in-charge of the POWs working on the Japanese monument was Col. Yasugi Tamura. When Lt. Nekemoto informed him of this wish, he was agreeable to the idea and promised to seek permission from the 5th Division's commander to not only allow the POWs to organise search parties but also to construct their own monument. At first, the general did not agree to the building of the POW monument, but after a heated discussion with Col. Tamura, he finally relented. He wanted to exploit this idea for Japanese propaganda purposes, to let the world and Singapore "appreciate and respect the hospitality of the Japanese military".

The POWs sent out search parties and cremated several bodies which they found. They built a 15-ft wooden cross which was located just behind the Japanese monument.

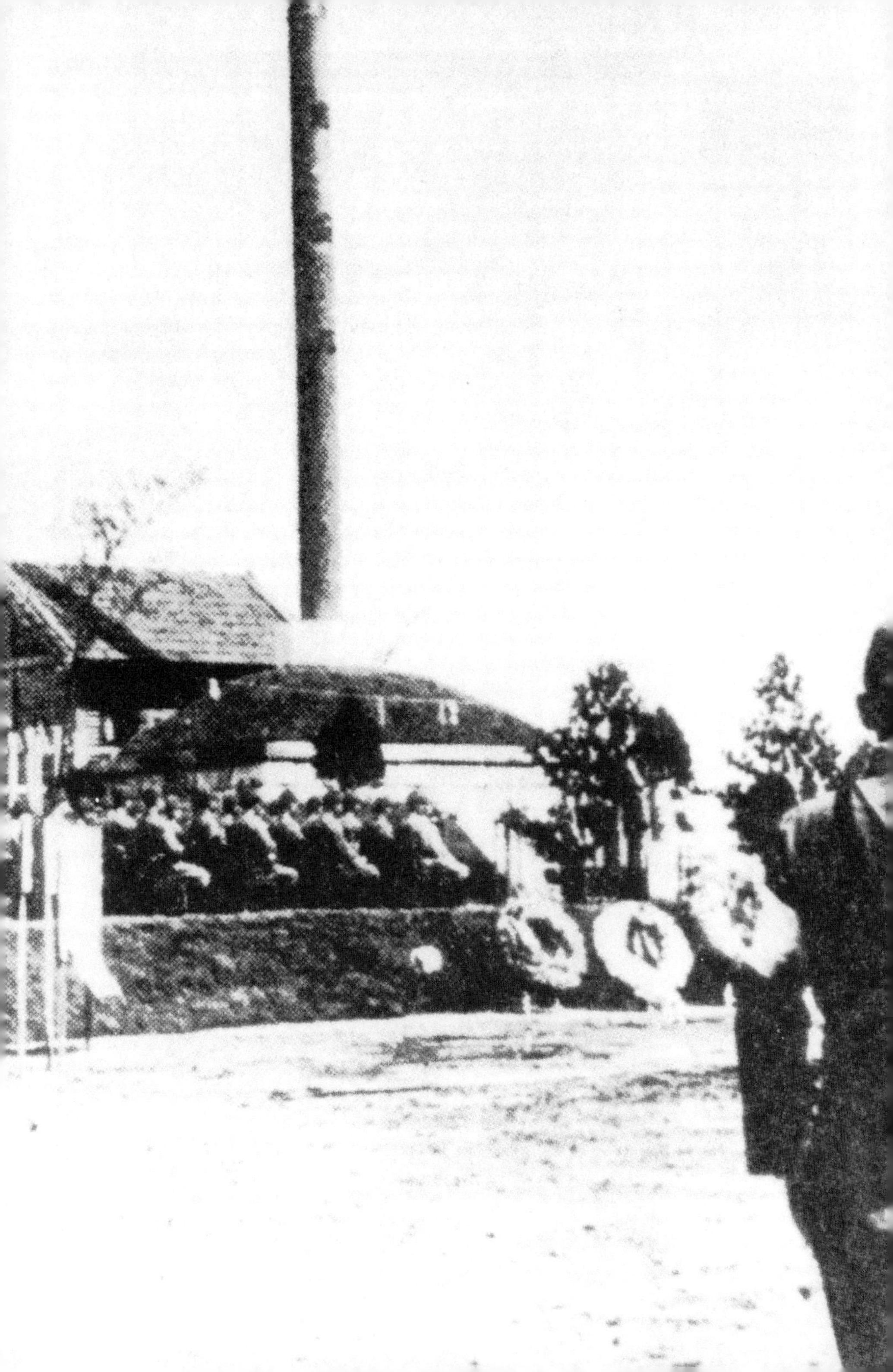

At the end of the war, Shonan Chureito was destroyed by the Japanese. The ashes of the more than 10,000 Japanese soldiers kept at Shonan Chureito were removed and placed in a tombstone in the Japanese Cemetery Park, together with the ashes of other Japanese troops that had previously been kept in a temple in Bencoolen Street.

Right: The steep steps leading up to the hilltop.

Page 50 below: The POW memorial on Bukit Batok.

Page 51: The Japanese honoured their dead as fallen heroes and stored their ashes in the memorial.

The unveiling of this cross was held on the same day as that of the Japanese monument. On 7 Dec 1942, "Shonan Chureito" was unveiled with a lot of media fanfare. After the unveiling of the Japanese monument, the crowd gathered in front of the British monument where it was unveiled by one of the POW camp commanders with a speech thanking the Japanese Army.

That night, the ashes of the Japanese dead were placed at the monument in a solemn ceremony. All lights near the monument were turned off and the sides of the stairs leading to the monument were lit by torches. Accompanied by a band, the ashes were reverently placed at the monument.

However, it is sad to note that after the Japanese surrender, both memorials were removed and replaced by a broadcasting tower. The steps are all that remain today. Upon the suggestion of a former POW, the Singapore Tourism Board erected a board at the foot of these steps. On the board are newspaper cuttings of news on the memorials, the letter written by the tourist and a picture showing where the memorials used to stand and what they looked like.

N4 Bukit Batok Hilltop

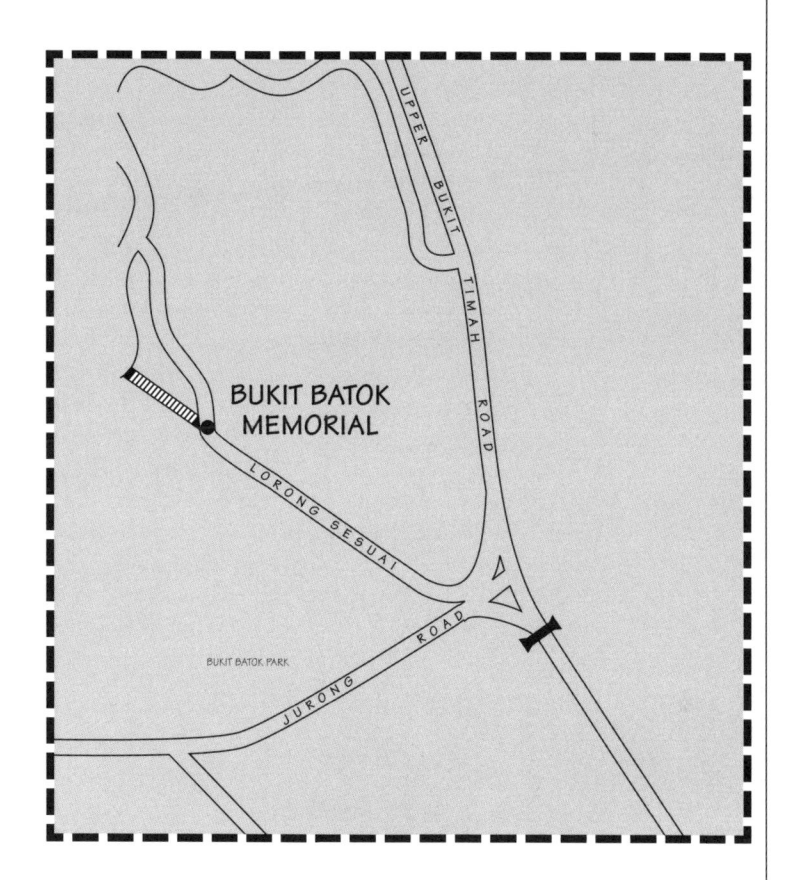

Notes

Situated on a hill, a long and steep staircase greets the visitor. The top of the hill is blocked by the transmitting tower. A few boulders are all that remain at the end of the stairs, the only reminder of the monuments' sad fate. The place is located along Lorong Sesuai which is a narrow road opposite Bukit Timah Fire Station.

Ford Motor Factory

As the Japanese invaded Malaya, a squadron of planes arrived from London to add to the strength of the Allied air force. They were to be assembled in Singapore, at the former Ford Factory. While they were being assembled, bombs were showered on this building by the Japanese who were informed of the arrival of the squadron. Several assembled planes and those still being assembled were all blown up, thus curtailing Singapore's air defence strength.

When Lt. Gen. Yamashita and his staff officers crossed the Straits in the pre-dawn hours of 10 Feb, he made his first headquarters in a rubber plantation north of Tengah airfield. On 13 Feb, he moved from this location to the Ford Motor Factory.

When the British decided to surrender on 15 Feb, a small group of representatives was sent to negotiate the surrender terms with Yamashita here. They were Lt. Gen. A. E. Percival (General Officer Commanding, HQ Malaya Command), Brig. Newbiggin (Percival's Chief Administrative Officer), Hugh Fraser (Acting Colonial Secretary) and Cyril Wild (a Japanese-speaking officer who also carried the surrender flag). Percival and his three officers arrived at 5.15 pm in a civilian car, flying the Union Jack and a white flag.

The deputation was met by Lt. Col. Sugita who led the surrender party to the factory. They were led into the factory's conference room to see Yamashita. Although Percival tried to stall for time, Yamashita demanded an immediate, unconditional surrender and pressed insistently for a ceasefire. Percival wanted to wait until the next morning before giving an answer, but Yamashita threatened to launch a massive attack on the city that very night. This would surely prove disastrous to the civilian population.

Faced with no alternative, Percival signed the surrender terms at 6.10 pm. After only seven days of battle, Singapore had ceased to exist as a British colony.

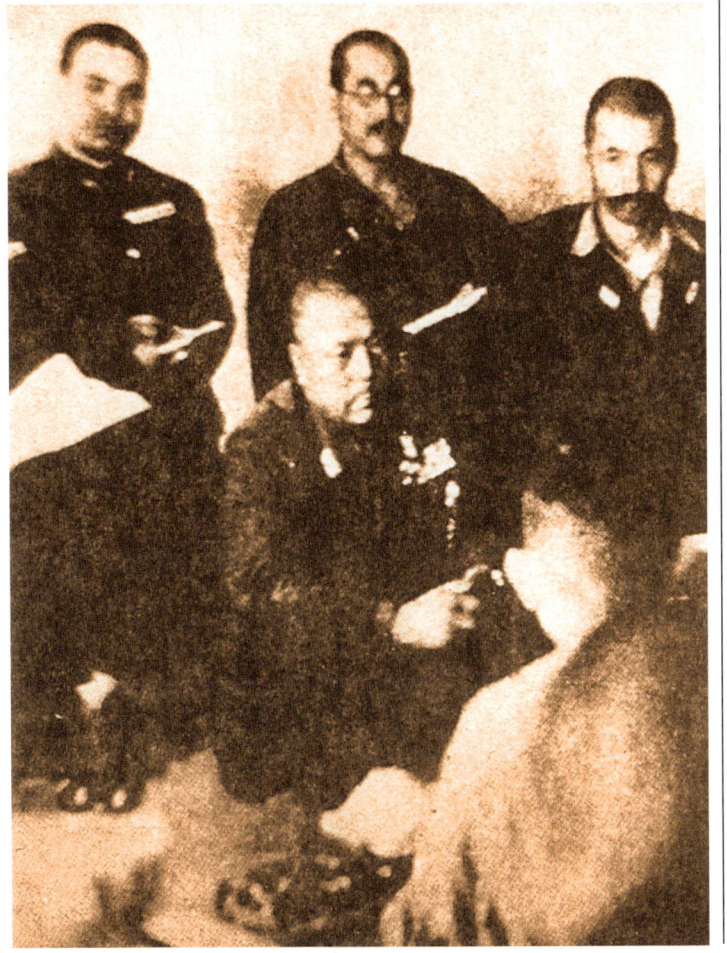

Left: For the first time, Lt. Gen. Percival meets his counterpart Lt. Gen. Yamashita. During negotiations, Yamashita pressed for the immediate and unconditional surrender of British forces. By then, Yamashita's troops were battle-weary and his ammunition and other supplies were also low.

Opposite Below: The British delegation marches into the Ford Motor Factory for that fateful meeting that sealed Singapore's fate.

Gen. Percival (extreme right) stands dejectedly beside Gen. Yamashita after the surrender.

N5 Ford Motor Factory

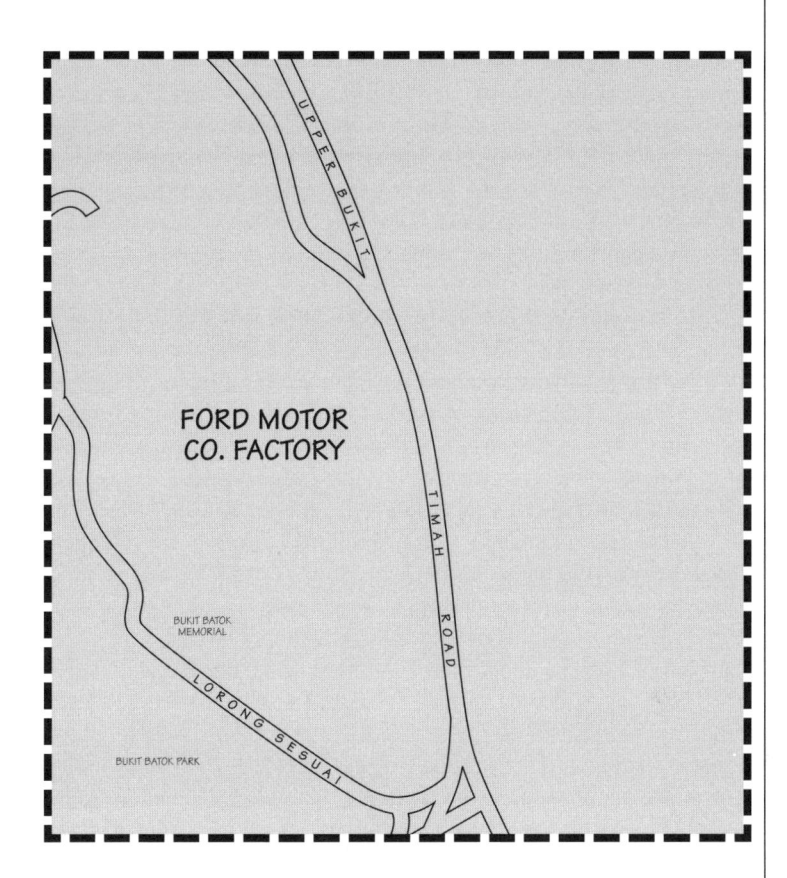

Notes

The place is located further up north of the Bukit Batok hilltop site along Upper Bukit Timah Road. Hong Leong Corporation occupies the premises. Access to the factory can be gained from the main road.

Bukit Timah Battle

The Battle for Bukit Timah accounted for the many skirmishes that were fought by the withdrawing British, Australian and Indian forces from the Causeway inland right up to the Bukit Timah Hill area. Bukit Timah Rd was the principal road in the southern half of Singapore. It was also the only road that linked the northern part of the island to the south. Bukit Timah became an area of immense tactical importance as the main military food supply depot was located just east of it.

By 7.30 pm on 9 Feb 1942, the Japanese had begun a frontal assault between the Causeway and Kranji. Unable to withstand the assault, the Malaya Command was forced to withdraw its forces further south. The capture of Bukit Timah, situated strategically in the centre of the island, would not only give the Japanese command of the north where a number of hillocks were situated, but also of the south as far down as Pasir Panjang village. 10 Feb was chosen by the Japanese for the attack on Bukit Timah. By then, the relentless Japanese pressure had already caused much confusion and panic in some sectors of the defence line, with several of the defending units withdrawing as a result of a series of miscommunications.

Meanwhile, the Japanese had started repairing the abandoned Causeway. By the morning of 10 Feb, the established Japanese forces on a hill near the Causeway had repeatedly repelled valiant attempts by the 27th Australian Brigade and the 8th and 12th Indian Infantry Brigades to stop the Japanese thrust. On 11 Feb, a counter offensive was planned for dawn the next day. This counter-attack was to be carried out by the 12th Indian Infantry Brigade in the north, the 15th Indian Infantry Brigade in the centre and the 22nd Australian Brigade in the south, with the 44th Indian Infantry Brigade in reserve.

However, by evening, the situation had worsened with the Japanese advancing in full force. At about 4 pm, Gen. Percival received news that the Japanese were approaching Bukit Timah. He immediately ordered the large reserve petrol depot east of the village destroyed. At about 8.15 pm, the defending troops came under attack. For the first time in the war, Japanese tanks made an appearance on the island. The Argylls hurriedly improvised two

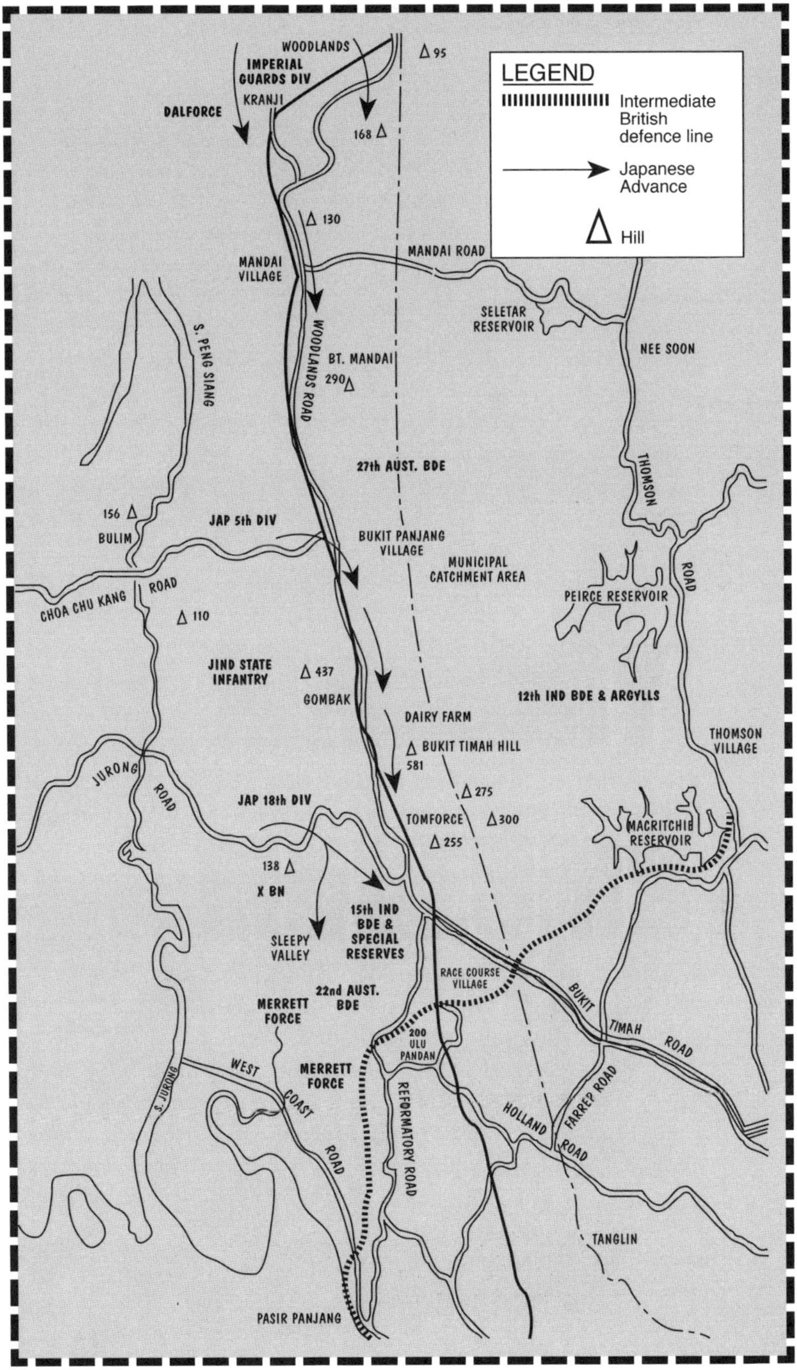
LEGEND
Intermediate British defence line
Japanese Advance
Hill
WOODLANDS
IMPERIAL GUARDS DIV
KRANJI
DALFORCE
95
168
130
MANDAI VILLAGE
MANDAI ROAD
SELETAR RESERVOIR
NEE SOON
S. PENG SIANG
WOODLANDS ROAD
BT. MANDAI
290
27th AUST. BDE
THOMSON
156
BULIM
JAP 5th DIV
BUKIT PANJANG VILLAGE
MUNICIPAL CATCHMENT AREA
ROAD
PEIRCE RESERVOIR
CHOA CHU KANG
ROAD
110
JIND STATE INFANTRY
437
GOMBAK
12th IND BDE & ARGYLLS
DAIRY FARM
BUKIT TIMAH HILL
581
THOMSON VILLAGE
JURONG
ROAD
275
JAP 18th DIV
TOMFORCE
300
255
MACRITCHIE RESERVOIR
138
X BN
15th IND BDE & SPECIAL RESERVES
SLEEPY VALLEY
RACE COURSE VILLAGE
BUKIT
TIMAH
ROAD
22nd AUST. BDE
MERRETT FORCE
200 ULU PANDAN
WEST
COAST
ROAD
MERRETT FORCE
S. JURONG
REFORMATORY ROAD
HOLLAND
ROAD
FARREP ROAD
TANGLIN
PASIR PANJANG

road blocks using all the vehicles and the few anti-tank mines that they had to deter the Japanese advance. When the leading Japanese tanks reached these points at about 10.30 pm, one was knocked out by the mines. However, the column of about 50 Japanese tanks supported by infantry broke through, forcing the Argylls and the 12th Brigade to withdraw to the east and through Dairy Farm, respectively.

On the same day, 11 Feb, at about 7.30 am, a company of British troops and the Special Reserve Battalion engaged the Japanese along Jurong Rd in a spirited counter-attack with their bayonets, driving them back and giving their commander, Brig. Coates, the opportunity to disengage. As a withdrawal down Jurong Rd was impossible, Brig. Coates split his force into three columns (one British, one Australian and one Indian) and set off in a south-easterly direction towards Reformatory Rd. While crossing Sleepy Valley, the columns came under heavy fire and suffered severe casualties. All cohesion was lost and eventually at about 1 pm, some 400 survivors — all that was left of a brigade some 1,500-strong — reached the 22nd Australian Brigade's positions.

Soldiers of the 12th and 15th Indian Brigades, 27th Australian Brigade, Special Reserves Battalion, Tomforce, Merrett Force, the Argylls, Jind State Infantry, X Battalion and the Dalforce, all faced the onslaught of the Japanese at various points along Bukit Timah. The soldiers bravely stood against the Japanese wherever possible, even though the odds were heavily stacked against them.

Page 59: Map showing the skirmishes and movements of the various troops along Bukit Timah.

Right: Japanese armour advancing into Bukit Timah.

N6 Bukit Timah Battle

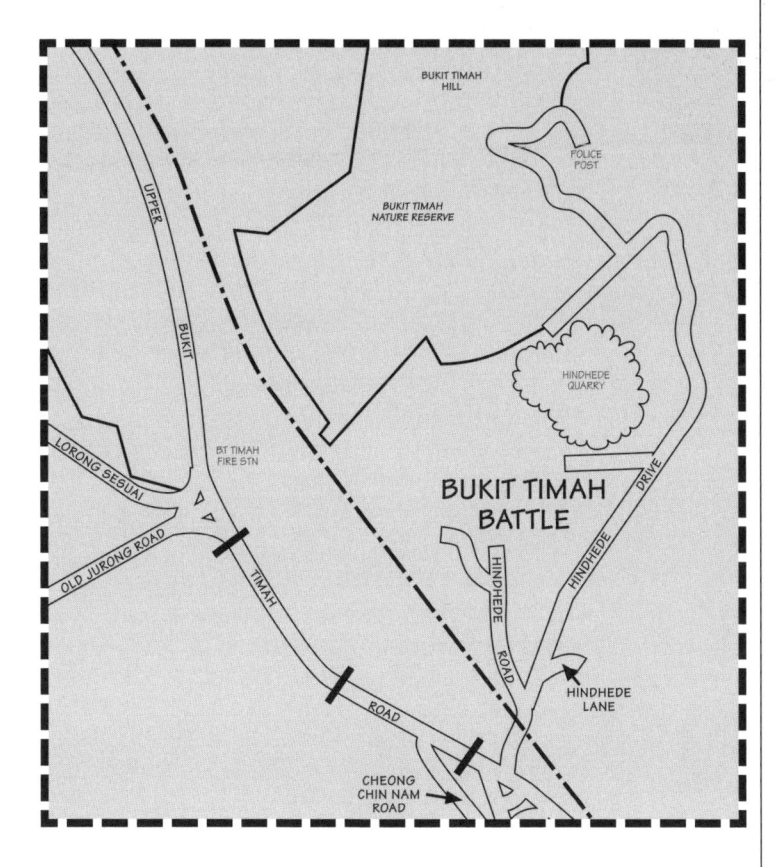

Notes

The Battle for Bukit Timah was actually a series of battles fought along the stretch of Bukit Timah Rd, from the junction with Choa Chu Kang Rd down to the junctions with Jurong and Reformatory (near Clementi) roads.

The painting depicts the heroic stand of the Malay Regiment on Pasir Panjang Ridge. The whole regiment stood their ground until almost to the last man.

THE CENTRAL TOUR

The Pasir Panjang Battle

Kent Ridge Park

On 13 Feb 1942, the Japanese concentrated their attack on the southern coastal area of Singapore, especially Pasir Panjang Ridge. The ridge was defended bitterly by the British for two reasons. It overlooked Singapore to the north and it gave access to the Alexandra area where the main ammunition depots, the British Military Hospital and other installations were grouped.

Here, the Japanese 18th Division fought a bitter battle with the 1st and 2nd Battalion of the Malay Regiment. The ferocious fight put up by the Malay Regiment was specially mentioned in Gen. Percival's Despatch on the Operations of Malaya Command from 8 Dec 1941 to 15 Feb 1942 (Second Supplement, London Gazette. Friday, 20 Feb 1948). The Despatch reads: "After two hours of heavy shelling and mortaring, it (the Japanese) attacked the Malay Regiment which was holding this feature (Pasir Panjang Ridge). The latter fought magnificently, but suffered heavy casualties, and by the afternoon the enemy had reached the Gap, a dominating position where the Buona Vista Road crosses the ridge ..."

The rapid Japanese advancement resulted in the Malay Regiment (consisting of two battalions) taking up new positions facing inland. The regiment had to lie in the open among low scrub day and night along the line of Ayer Rajah Rd and, later, the Pasir Panjang Ridge.

On the morning of 13 Feb 1942, the Japanese bombarded the ridge with aerial support, and heavy mortar and artillery fire. "C" Coy was defending Pasir Panjang Village when the Japanese 18th Division turned their attention westwards after attacking the ridge. The Malay Regiment's stubborn resistance stalled the Japanese advance and forced them to withdraw for the night.

At midnight, "C" Coy was allotted a new defence position near the eastern edge of Pasir Panjang Ridge, a position known as Point 226. The battle that took place there later came to be known as the "Battle of Opium Hill" as it was near the government opium factory. This battle revealed the bravery of "C" Coy for, though they suffered heavy casualties and were greatly outnumbered, they held on to their position and fought back, supported by fire from the remaining 9.2-inch and 6-inch guns of Faber Fire Command.

Cpt. H.R. Rix became "C" Coy commander after the death of its officer. He arranged for his platoons to provide an all-round defence of the ridge. There were no trenches, no food and water supplies forthcoming and the ammunition stock of the company amounted to a Bofors anti-tank gun, a 2-inch mortar, Lewis guns, hand grenades and rifles. Cpt. Rix's bravery spurred his men as he visited them at intervals from his HQ to the northwest despite Japanese bombardments.

The Japanese assault on Opium Hill to dislodge the Malay Regiment started with a ruse in the early afternoon of 14 Feb. A group of Japanese soldiers disguised themselves as Punjabi troops and advanced forward in a friendly gesture. Lt. Adnan, whose troops were facing north, was not fooled and opened fire killing and wounding about 20 Japanese. The Japanese then went on an all-round assault and overwhelmed the Malay Regiment.

The reprisals of the Japanese were quick and brutal. Cpt. Rix was killed along with 12 Malay soldiers who died fighting beside him. Lt. Adnan was shot, bayoneted and his body hung up from a nearby tree by the Japanese. No one was allowed to remove his body. Six of his men were captured, tied up and bayoneted, but one managed to escape by crawling away in the dark. Lt. Abbas, who was put in charge of the southeast sector of the ridge, fought bravely until only about six men survived uninjured. He then led these few men on a

Above: A westward view from the Pasir Panjang Ridge showing the area from which the Japanese approached Singapore City.

Opposite Below: A mortar team from the Malay Regiment during an exercise.

Fortress Singapore

desperate withdrawal to the Battalion HQ.

They were pursued by the Japanese and, when encountering a wide drain filled with burning oil, they had no choice but to jump across it. Four exhausted soldiers failed to clear the drain and two were burnt to death. Two others were pulled out by Lt. Abbas and his men, but had to be left behind as they were unable to continue because of their burns. Finally, only Lt. Abbas and three of his men reached the Battalion HQ situated on a low hill near Alexandra Barracks after dark to report the entire wipeout of the regiment.

The magnificent stand put up by the Malay Regiment merits an honoured mention in the history of our nation.

Above: *This pillbox, located next to the Shell petrol station along Pasir Panjang Road, is one of the last remaining pillboxes in Singapore. In 1942, the pillbox overlooked a stretch of beach. Soldiers taking aim with their guns through the gun-slots were well protected from enemy shelling.*

Right: *The Straits Times commemorates the 25th anniversary of the Pasir Panjang Battle.*

The fire and death on 'Opium Hill'

FROM WAR DESPATCHES AND MEMORIES OF THE FEW WHO SURVIVED THIS BRUTAL ENGAGEMENT THIS STORY IS TOLD

by
HAJI MUBIN SHEPPARD

C1 Kent Ridge Park

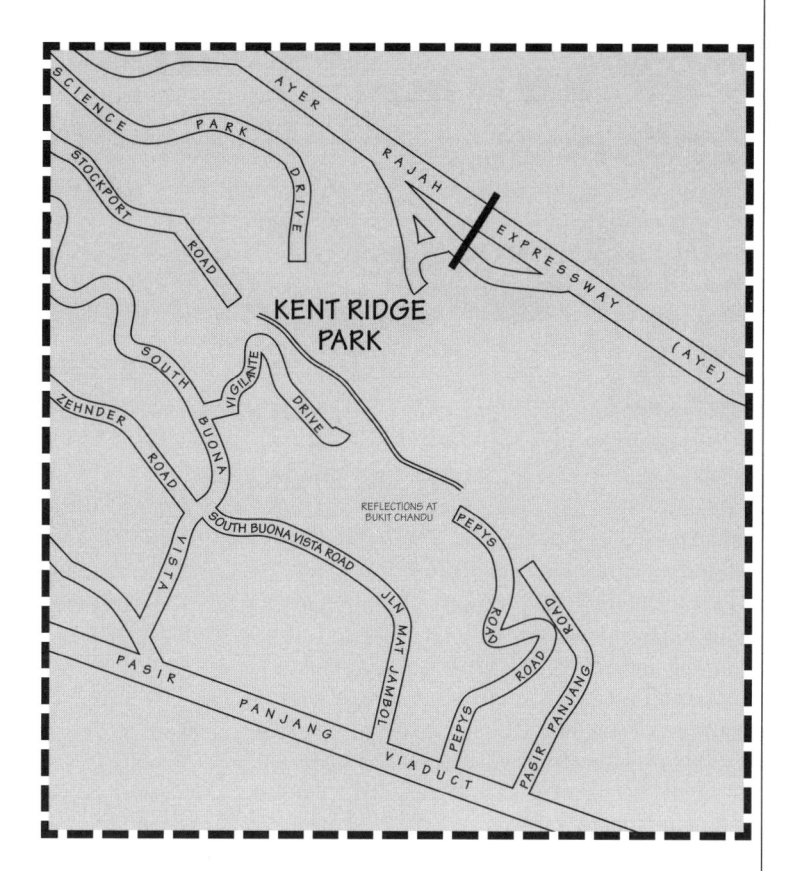

Notes

The park is quite big and a stroll through it will give readers a good view of the Pasir Panjang area. The hill is easily accessible but is quite steep in some places. You can also visit the "Reflections at Bukit Chandu", a WWII Interpretative Centre. Located at 31-K Pepys Road, this centre focuses on the Malay Regiment and their courageous battle for Pasir Panjang Ridge. The centre is accessible via a footpath along the ridge.

Fortress Singapore

Labrador Park

When planning for the defence of Singapore, the British constructed defences mainly along the southern coast in anticipation of a seaward attack. Since the north was protected by the mainland of Malaysia and the northeast by the fortified Naval Base, the British saw no need to build defences on the northern shores of Singapore. The construction of permanent beach defences was started in 1936.

Labrador Park was one of the areas where defences were prepared. The Labrador Battery was built in 1939 and manned by two 6-inch guns which were positioned facing south. The Battery came under the operation of the 7th Coast Artillery Regiment, which received orders from the Faber Fire Command led by Brig. A.D. Curtiss. The guns had a range of over 10 miles, and could fire a 102-lb shell with a 31-lb cartridge. During the Battle for Singapore, these guns assisted the Malay Regiment in their 48-hour struggle against the Japanese 18th Division by firing high explosive shells at enemy troops advancing along the coastal road through Pasir Panjang. The guns were destroyed before Singapore fell in 1942 but one was repaired and used by the Japanese during the Occupation years. Although these guns have been removed, their positions are still visible by the two large dome-shaped cemented areas. Pillboxes (tiny box-like defence structures in which two riflemen can stand) can also be found in Labrador Park, all facing south.

It has long been speculated that there are several tunnels and bunkers beneath the Battery which provided easy access to Fort Siloso, Connaught and Serapong on Sentosa Island and Fort Silinsing on Pulau Brani. The Battery does consist of bunkers that were sealed in the 1950s and thus have been unexplored. The entrance to the bunker is still visible from the outside and many of the gun emplacements are still left intact.

68

The Central Tour

C2 Labrador Park

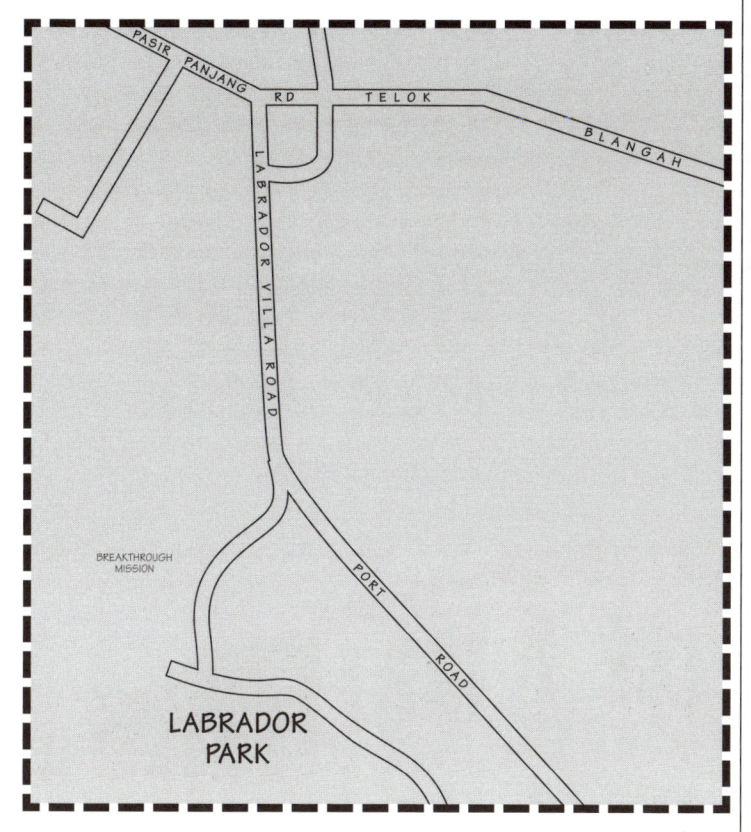

Opposite Below: A fire direction tower, left intact since it met its fate almost 50 years ago. All the battery emplacements still remain and the area has been transformed into a lush and peaceful garden park.

Notes

One of the vital links of Fortress Singapore, Labrador Park is filled with relics. The gun emplacements and fire direction towers are still visible. Here you can almost feel the sense of urgency during the hurried preparation for war. The place is located opposite PSA Building along Pasir Panjang Road.

Fortress Singapore

Alexandra Hospital

As a result of the ferocious fighting in the Kent Ridge grounds, some Japanese soldiers stormed into Alexandra Hospital on 14 Feb 1942 on a killing rampage. There were claims that Indian soldiers had set up machine guns in the hospital grounds and fired first at the Japanese.

The Japanese entered the hospital from the rear, and killed a British officer, Lt. Weston, who was carrying a white flag to meet them. They went through the hospital grounds bayoneting everyone they could find, regardless of whether they were patients or medical personnel. Personal accounts recalled that the Japanese soldiers were very excitable or were ignorant of the Red Cross armbands worn by the hospital staff.

They even intruded into an operating theatre while an operation was in progress and killed everyone including the patient (a young soldier, Cpl. Holden) on the table. Some managed to escape death by falling to the floor and pretending to be dead.

Massacre!!

The Central Tour

Left: The Alexandra Hospital is a modern health care centre today.

Opposite Below: The Alexandra Hospital then, was used as a military hospital by the British during the Malayan Campaign.

Nearly 200 patients and staff were collected from the main building and mercilessly crammed into the old servants' quarters behind the hospital. The quarters consisted of several tiny rooms in which 50 to 70 people were squeezed together. They were tied in groups of four and five and packed so tightly together that they had to stand the whole night, with some patients raising their arms over their head to make more room. Because they were so closely packed, they had to urinate on each other. They were also denied food and water, and many men died in the night.

About eight men tried to escape when a shell struck the roof of the building, blowing open the doors and windows. The Japanese opened fire and killed five of them, but those who escaped were about the only ones ever seen alive from the 200 or so in the bungalow. At intervals, groups were brought out to be killed.

Apparently, Yamashita was unaware of the massacre. The following day, a Japanese general toured the hospital and distributed tinned fruits, all the while apologising profusely for the brutality of the Japanese soldiers and assured the staff that they would not be further molested. He also ordered the execution of the Japanese soldiers responsible for the massacre, within the hospital grounds.

The entrance to Alexandra Hospital witnessed some of the worst massacres in Singapore.

C3 Alexandra Hospital

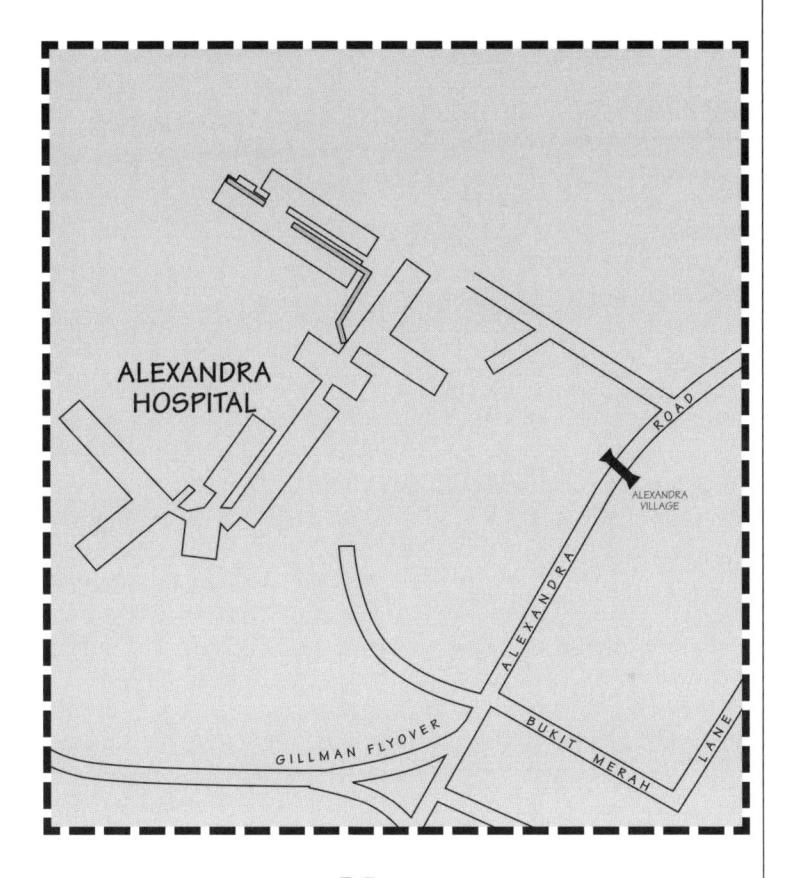

Notes

A modern hospital, Alexandra Hospital still retains its colonial structure.

Fortress Singapore

Singapore General Hospital

Student Tragedy

On 14 Feb 1942, 11 medical and dental students of the King Edward VII College of Medicine were killed by Japanese shelling. The tragedy occurred when about 25 students took part in a burial ceremony for one of their fellow students, Yoong Tat Sin, a fourth-year medical student.

Yoong Tat Sin had been fatally injured by Japanese shelling while on duty at the Tan Tock Seng Hospital on the morning of 14 Feb. Although he was rushed to the Outram Road General Hospital (as the Singapore General Hospital was then known) for an emergency operation, he died soon after.

That same evening, the medical and dental students of the College of Medicine decided to give Yoong a proper burial within the grounds of the hospital and about 25 students accompanied the coffin to the burial ground. The burial site the students had chosen already had five trenches dug out earlier for air raid purposes and they decided to convert one of these trenches into a grave for Yoong. However, as the grave was being prepared, Japanese gunners, who had sighted the students, began pouring a heavy barrage of shells at them.

Some of the students at the burial ground managed to flee to safety towards the College building. But the rest of the students who were left behind only had time to leap into the trenches and Yoong's grave. Eight were killed instantaneously while another

74

IN MEMORIAM

They shall not grow old, as we that are left grow old.
Age shall not weary them, nor years condemn.

Page 74 (Below): The College of Medicine was then known as the King Edward VII College of Medicine.

Page 75: The 11 students who were killed by Japanese shelling. Yoong Tat Sin is the second picture in the second row.

Below: The Federated Malay States hostel where the medical students stayed.

five were wounded. Two of the wounded later died from their injuries. Only two students managed to escape injury.

Those who were killed instantaneously were given a burial on the morning of 16 Feb 1942 in the trenches where they fell.

When the British returned after the end of the war, the burial ground was flattened. A cross commemorating British soldiers and civilian war dead along Hospital Drive marks the spot near where two of the slain students were buried.

On 22 Oct 1948, a War Memorial Plaque with the names of the 11 slain students inscribed on it was unveiled by Dr G. V. Allen, then the principal of the Medical College, in the presence of the governor of Singapore, Sir Franklin Gimson. The plaque was first hung in Harrower Hall but over the years, it has been moved twice. Today, it hangs in the foyer of the College of Medicine Building, close to the burial ground of the slain students.

C4 **Singapore General Hospital**

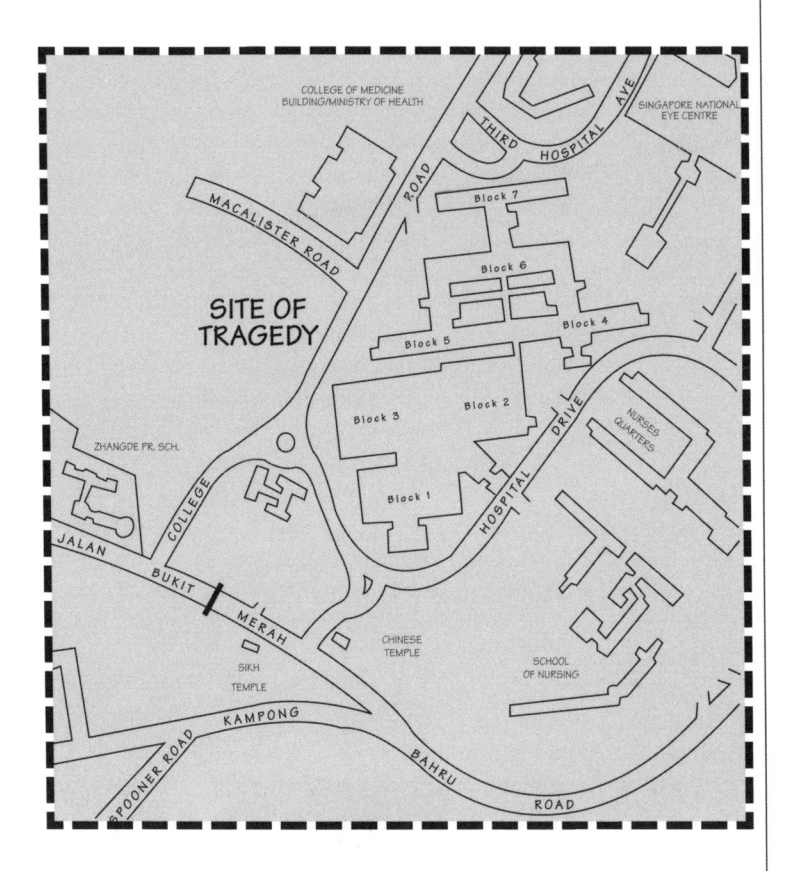

Notes

Most of the pre-war low buildings of the hospital have given way to the modern multi-storeyed blocks of today. The College of Medicine building is one of the few buildings left over from the pre-war period while the cross along Hospital Drive is the only reminder of the war.

Padang & City Hall

On 17 Feb 1942, the entire European population was assembled here at about 10 am for inspection and questioning. Military personnel were separated from the civilians. Among the civilians, the men were separated from the women and children. They were told to bring clothes for ten days and that food would be provided. The senior government officials led by Sir Shenton Thomas were also gathered at the Padang. Sir Thomas was especially singled out for humiliation and was made to walk to their first camp in Katong, though some senior officials were allowed to drive there.

After waiting for two hours under the hot sun, the civilians were told to walk to Katong and that food would not be provided. This was most distressing news and some civilians went scrounging for whatever food was available. The military personnel were later forced to march off to Selarang Barracks, 22 km away, or to Changi Camp.

The City Hall was used by the Japanese as the Office of Syonan Municipality (Syonan Tokubetsu Shi) during the Occupation. This Special City Government comprised four major bureaus: General Affairs, Public Welfare, Public Works and Police. A few civilian Japanese officials helped to run it.

On 6 July 1943, a parade by the Indian National Army was held at the Padang in honour of the visit of Gen. Tojo, the Japanese Premier. While the VIPs viewed the scene from the balcony of the

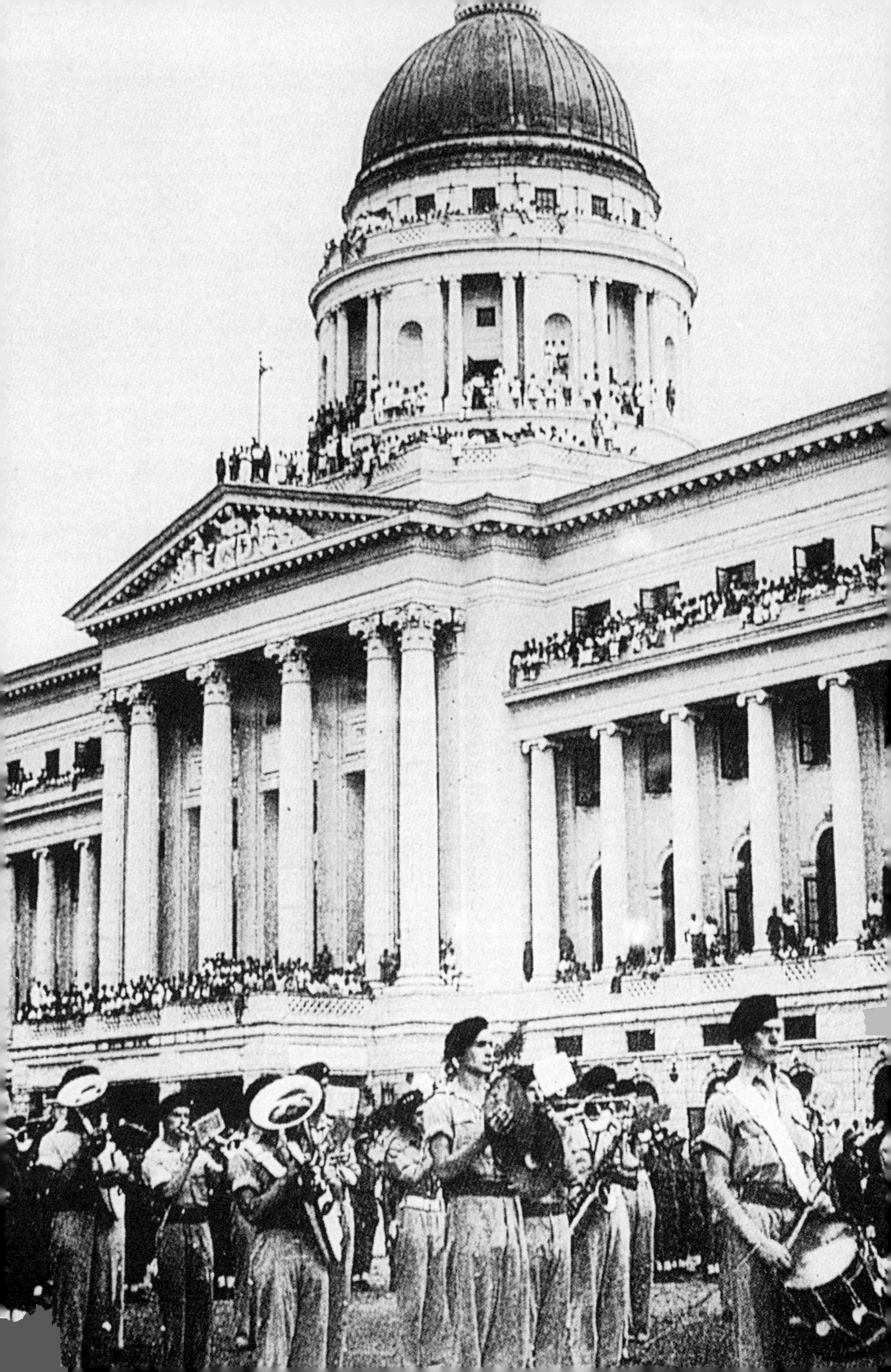

Fortress Singapore

Page 78 Below: Within the City Hall, Lt. Gen. Itagaki, Supreme Commander of the Japanese Forces in the Southern Regions, signs the Surrender Document.

Page 79: Outside City Hall, there was an air of quiet expectancy. When the British band struck the tune of "God Save the King", a scene of tumultuous celebration erupted on the Padang. In the background stands the Supreme Court of Singapore.

Right: Vice-Admiral Lord Louis Mountbatten (in front), Supreme Allied Commander of Southeast Asia, raises his cap to acknowledge victory over the Japanese.

City Hall, light tanks, gun-tractors and troops paraded smartly on the Padang field.

The Indian National Army was formed with help from the Japanese who used it for propaganda purposes. Subhas Chandra Bose, the Supreme Commander of the Army, was also the president of the Indian Independence League. The League was formed to rally support for the liberation of India from British rule.

When Chandra Bose declared himself head of the Provisional Government of India on 21 Oct 1943, he was supported by the Japanese government, China's Wang Chin Wei's government, the Philippines, Thailand, Manchukuo (Manchuria), Germany and Italy. A large rally was held on the Padang three days later on 24 Oct 1943 where Chandra Bose declared war against Britain and the United States.

On 12 Sep 1945, at this same site, the local population gathered, this time to witness the surrender of the Japanese to the British. The Japanese, represented by Lt. Gen. Itagaki, Supreme Commander of the Japanese Forces in the Southern regions, signed the Surrender Document in the Council Chamber at the City Hall. It was accepted by Lord Louis Mountbatten, Supreme Allied Commander of the Southeast Asian Command.

C5 Padang & City Hall

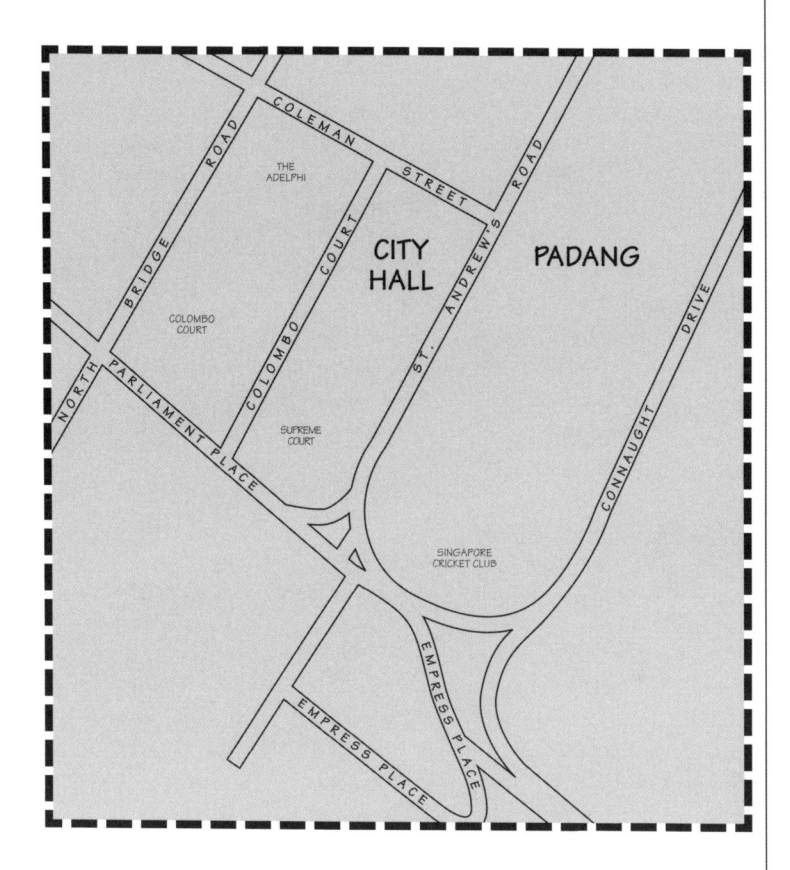

Notes

Through time, the Padang and City Hall have become ageless. They continue to be an inspiration for modern Singapore. Easy access gives visitors a chance to walk on the very ground where history was made.

Kandahar Street

After the war, the Japanese wanted to get rid of all anti-Japanese elements. The Chinese were especially targeted because many of them actively supported China in their war against Japan by sending money back and boycotting Japanese goods. The especially ferocious fight put up by the Dalforce against the Japanese gave Yamashita more reason to hate the Chinese. The Second Field Kempeitai under Lt. Col. Satoru Oishi was put in charge of this operation known as "Sook Ching." Literally translated, it means "to eliminate", and it became a massacre of the Chinese.

On 18 Feb 1942, Chinese males between 18 and 50 years of age were instructed to assemble at five major "registration camps" around Singapore to be screened. The five camps were at:

a. the open area near Jalan Besar Stadium and the north end of Arab St,
b. the eastern end of River Valley Rd near the Clemenceau Ave junction,
c. the open area near Tanjong Pagar Police Station,
d. the rubber factory near the junction of Kallang and Geylang Rd, and
e. the open area off Paya Lebar Rd.

The Chinese were instructed to gather at the camps without any explanation. They were assembled at the camps over a few days. Some were informed that they would only be away for a few days, and were then herded to certain areas — under the merciless sun — without food, water or shelter.

Many were dragged out from their homes at bayonet point. Old men, women and children were mistakenly rounded up to some of these camps. At the camps, many were wilfully selected to their deaths. No standard selection procedure was followed. In some camps, women and children were released while the men (sometimes even boys) were herded into trucks and driven away, never to be seen again. In other camps, people were condemned at will; sometimes entire families were sent to their deaths. Some were selected because they signed their names in English or they were former servants of European households. Those who belonged to the following categories were in exceptional danger of being sent to their deaths:

The Central Tour

1. Those with any connection to the China Relief Fund which provided the money for China's war of resistance against Japan.
2. Rich men who would most likely donate generously to the Relief Fund.
3. Those with links to Tan Kah Kee, an active member of the Fund.
4. Newspapermen, schoolmasters and high school students whose counterparts in China had antagonised the Japanese.
5. Hainan Island natives who were suspected to be communists by the Japanese.
6. Recent settlers to Malaya who must have left China because of dislike of the Japanese.
7. Men with tattoo marks who must be members of secret societies.
8. Members of the military force, be it volunteer or regular. They might rise up against the Japanese again.
9. Civil servants, for they were likely to be pro-British.

A Sook Ching concentration point along North Bridge Rd. These buildings can still be seen today.

Fortress Singapore

The camps were run according to the whims and fancy of the Japanese commandants. One camp lasted six hours while another dragged on for six days. Almost a thousand were detained randomly at one camp while there were none detained at another.

One thing was certain though, of those who were selected and detained, very few were ever seen again. Most were brought to the beaches off Ponggol, Changi and Sentosa and executed. Only a handful survived the ordeal. Survivors recounted how they were tied together, made to line up in a row on the beach and machine-gunned. When the guns stopped, the Japanese would come round and bayonet the fallen bodies.

Lucky ones who passed the screening were issued with identification passes in the form of the Chinese word "examined" rubber-stamped on their clothes or bodies. Many cut out that portion of the cloth to use as a pass against further harassment, and those who had it on their bodies went as far as not cleaning the area where the stamp was. However, many who had been cleared were rearrested at the slightest excuse and then executed. Estimates of those who perished in Sook Ching were officially recorded as 6,000, but as many as 25,000 to 50,000 are believed to have died. Of those who perished, the youngest was 12 while the oldest was 58.

Identification documents issued at the Sook Ching interrogation centres.

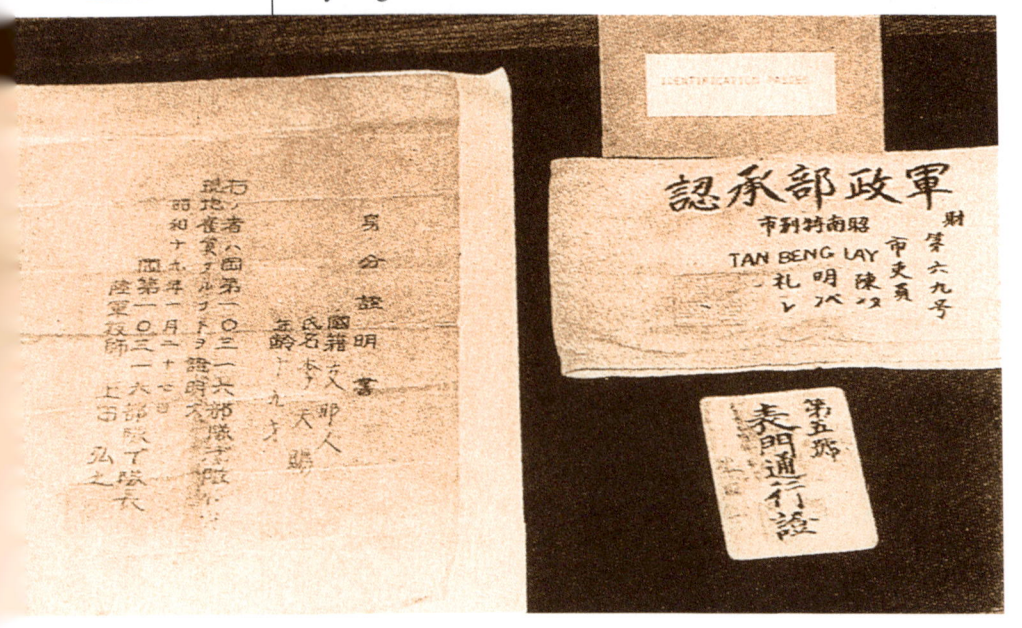

C6 Kandahar Street

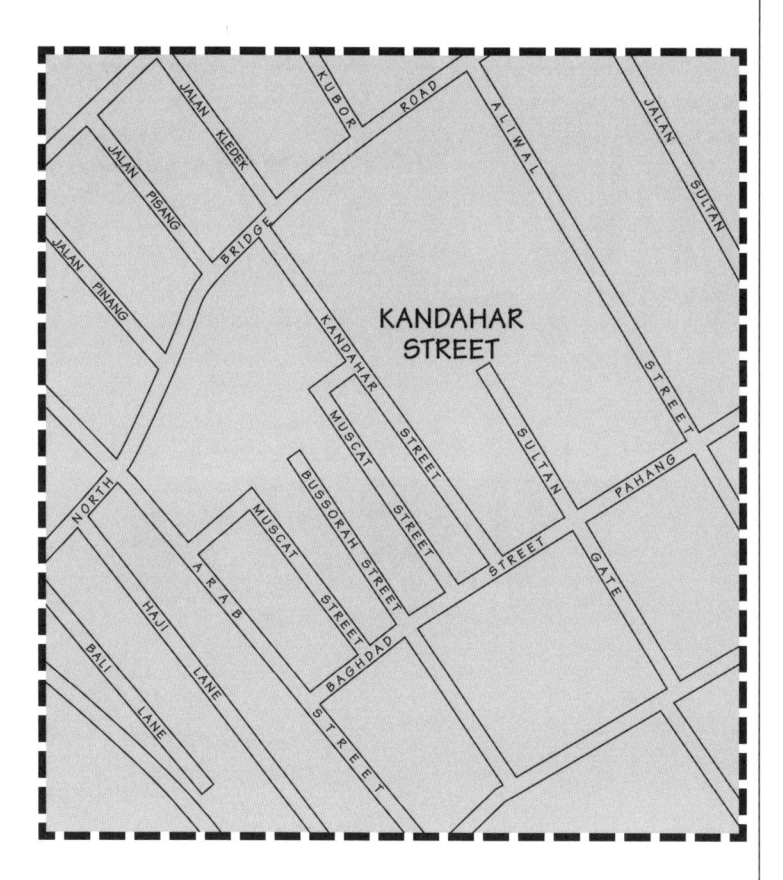

Notes

Kandahar Street is a very busy road and access is sometimes difficult. You can, however, see the original buildings that are shown in the photograph.

Fortress Singapore

Fort Canning Park

Within this hill lies a deep and complicated network of military bunkers. Behind the locked doors (Percival Rd) on the sides of the hill are tunnels which converge at the centre of the hill. Here, Percival's headquarters were located. The underground bunkers, about 40 rooms in all, were never fully made use of until the last days before the British surrender.

On 15 Feb 1942, at 9.30 am, Percival held a conference here with all his commanders to discuss the deteriorating water supply and the worsening administrative situation. Percival wanted to launch a massive assault to recapture vital Japanese-occupied locations. He consulted his field commanders on this possibility, but his commanders were against the idea as the troops were demoralised and disorganised. By a unanimous vote, the inevitable decision was made to surrender.

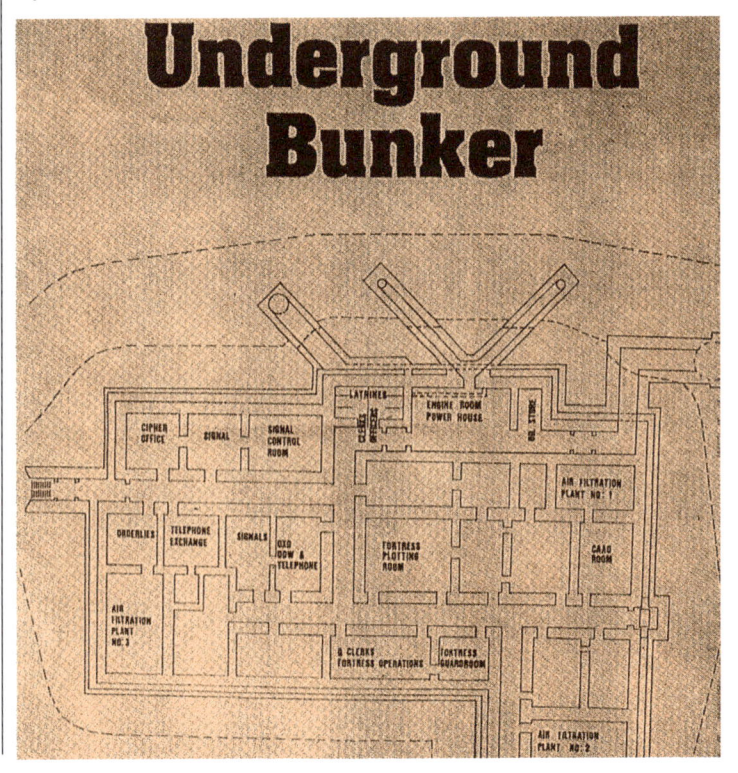

Underground Bunker

The Central Tour

C7 Fort Canning Park

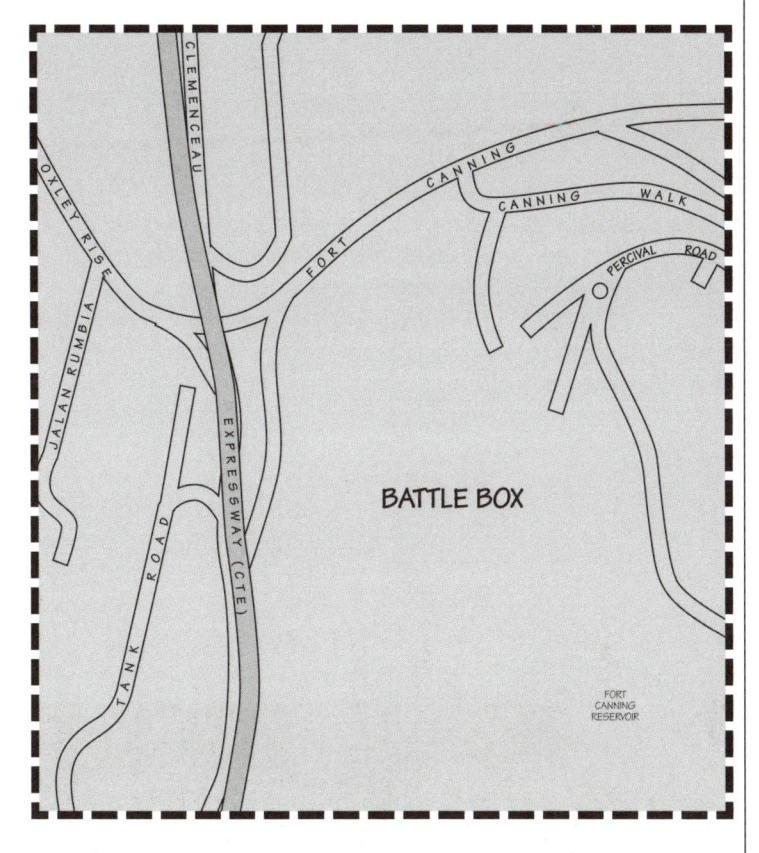

Opposite Below:
Plan of the Battlebox, the HQ of the British Malaya Command during the last days of the war.

Notes

This bunker is now open to the public as part of the "Battle Box". Through the use of audio-visual effects and animatronics, visitors are brought back in time to the fateful morning of 15 Feb 1942.

Fort Siloso

Fort Siloso lies at the northwestern tip of Sentosa Island. Built in the 1880s, Fort Siloso, Fort Connaught and Fort Serapong were located on Blakang Mati Island, now known as Sentosa, as part of the coastal defences of Singapore.

During the 1930s, with the clouds of war looming, Fort Siloso underwent a major redevelopment. At Siloso point, a 12-pounder quick-firing gun was installed. This gun was provided with a three-storey directional tower and three stilted searchlight posts. Two machine gun posts, two searchlight posts and an operational control tower were also added at various locations. At the entrance of the fort, a guardhouse was erected, and two twin Lewis anti-aircraft machine guns replaced the l0-inch gun emplaced near the fort's entrance. To accommodate large supply boats, the Siloso Jetty was extended.

By 1941, Blakang Mati was a self-sufficient fortress with its own fresh water supply, the reservoir being located underground below the concrete structures and fortifications of Mount Serapong. Armament of the batteries on the island included Fort Serapong with two 6-inch guns, Fort Connaught with three 9.2-inch guns and Fort Siloso with two 6-inch guns and one 12-pounder.

Though under heavy Japanese air attack, Connaught, Siloso and

Serapong engaged the enemy both on land and at sea. Misfortune, however, befell the gunners at Fort Siloso. On the evening of 10 Feb, the gunners of the overrun Pasir Laba Battery were escaping via sea in an attempt to get back to British lines. Mistaking the identity of these retreating men, the gunners of Fort Siloso opened fire on their escaping craft.

By 13 Feb, Labrador Battery was put out of action, but the defenders on Blakang Mati still fought gallantly. On 13 and 14 Feb, Fort Siloso assisted in the destruction of the oil installation on Pulau Bukom and Pulau Sebarok, to prevent their falling into Japanese hands. The 9.2-inch guns at Fort Connaught also fired their entire ammunition on Japanese troops in Tengah airfield on 15 Feb and caused much damage. When news of the surrender reached Blakang Mati on the 15th, the remaining guns were destroyed by the British.

Fort Siloso became a POW camp for both military and civilian personnel. Today, it is the only complete fort existing in Singapore. The fort also serves as a repository for the various guns that formed part of Singapore's coastal defence, consisting of coastal guns from 1880 to 1940.

Above: Fort Siloso commands a perfect view of the entrance to the port of Singapore.

Opposite Below: One of the big guns that protected the southern coasts of Singapore. During the war these guns were turned around and fired at advancing Japanese troops.

Fortress Singapore

C8 Fort Siloso

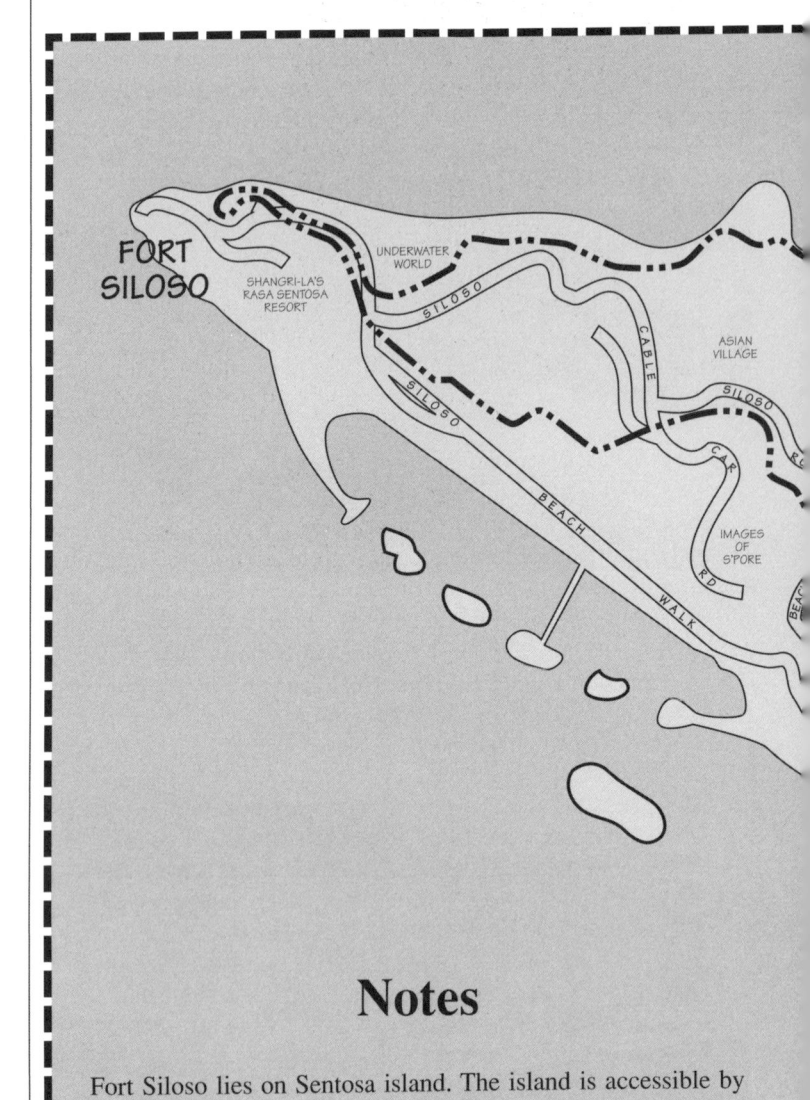

Notes

Fort Siloso lies on Sentosa island. The island is accessible by bus or cable car. On reaching the island, take either the island bus or monorail to the Fort.

The Central Tour

Changi Prison is a grim reminder of WWII. Here, as many men died from disease and deprivation as from starvation of the spirit and soul.

THE EASTERN TOUR

Fortress Singapore

Changi Prison

Changi prison was originally built for 600 people. On 17 Feb 1942, just after Singapore fell, about 3,000 European civilian prisoners were made to walk to Katong from the Padang. They were housed in some houses near the Sea View Hotel. The men were moved to Changi Prison first, followed by the women and children a week later. Except for the old and pregnant, everybody had to walk the seven miles to the prison. They carried whatever belongings they could in prams, boxes and their hands.

The Japanese wanted to humiliate the Europeans and let the local population witness how their great colonial masters had fallen, thus the long march on the streets. However, far from the jeering crowds expected, the locals were sympathetic and made attempts, at the risk of their lives, to relieve the misery of the Europeans through offers of food and water.

The march of the women and children took one whole day, and they reached the prison only at 4 pm. Singing along the way, they were joined in by the men within the prison walls when they finally reached sight of it. The women and children were kept together away from the men and only allowed to meet on special occasions like Christmas.

At the same time, military POWs were housed in Changi military barracks outside the prison walls occupying places like the officers' bungalows, barrack blocks, storerooms or simply makeshift tents set up on available spaces. By 18 Feb, these men who consisted of

"A Hellish Existence"

The Eastern Tour

Chinese members of the local volunteer regiment, Indian Army officers and Allied soldiers numbered around 52,200. But the numbers fluctuated over the captive years as men died or were taken away to make up labour forces building various shrines and the infamous Death Railway.

In the beginning, the Japanese placed no restrictions on movement within the Changi area. In Mar 1942, however, the internees were required to wire in their own areas corresponding to each military division, and movement became limited as Japanese soldiers and Sikh guards patrolled the area.

In May 1944, the civilian POWs were moved out of Changi Prison to Sime Road camp to make way for 12,000 military POWs from Selarang and Robert Barracks. Only about 5,000 POWs were kept in the prison itself. The rest were housed in makeshift campsites outside the building. Conditions for the civilian and military POWs were extremely deplorable. Lack of food and proper sanitation caused many deaths. The Japanese rationed out rice with little tea, sugar, salt and an occasional morsel of meat and fish. Widespread dysentery caused many deaths. Vitamin deficiency manifested itself in the appearance of raw scrotums and tongues, and open sores on legs. Many also died of illnesses which were not treated, although drugs were available to the Japanese. For example, chronic diabetics died because the Japanese refused to issue insulin that was available. The doctors battled valiantly using what available drugs they could get hold of, but the cemetery in Changi kept filling up.

The prisoners tried to make the best of what was available. Within the prison walls, gardens sprouted and plays, dramas and concerts were staged. A school was set up for the children and a women's camp paper was published. The military POWs were especially ingenious. They organised lectures covering topics like communism, architecture, geography, etc. There was even a Changi University set up. Unfortunately, it was reduced to an Education Centre when its staff was depleted by the departure of working parties. Lecturers and teachers were discovered among officers with professional qualifications, and almost the entire staff of Raffles College were also interned in Changi. Stage groups performed a wide variety of programmes from Shakespeare to light musicals every week. These concerts were often attended by Japanese guards too.

Above: Located at the entrance leading to the Changi museum is a plaque mounted on a thick slab of concrete. The brass plaque is the handiwork of an Australian dentist, Dr Ross J. Bastiaan. It was laid down in Feb 1992 to commemorate the 50th anniversary of the battle for Singapore. The plaque shows a relief map of the Changi area and a sculptured replica of Changi prison, while the text describes the main events of the POW story.

Opposite Below: A reconstruction of the chapel at Changi. Masses were always packed as religion became the only solace for the men.

Workshops were set up where many homemade items were created using much creativity and imagination. Artificial legs were made for amputees from rubber trees and old filing cabinets. Homemade paper was made from pounded grass, water and potash. Latex was also tapped regularly from nearby rubber trees and urine used as a coagulant. The military POWs also made toys for the interned children during Christmas, using whatever materials they could find.

Clandestine short-wave radio sets were operated in many secret hideouts in and outside the prison walls by both civilians and military POWs. Smuggled parts were brought in, cleverly hidden in broom handles and other nooks and crevices. The Japanese conducted random spot checks and when any of these radio sets were found, the Kempeitai would torture the victim mercilessly. One such incident of torture occurred during the Double Tenth Incident when an Allied raiding party successfully entered Singapore harbour on a sabotage mission. Fifty-seven civilian internees were removed by the Kempeitai for interrogation. Fifteen men died as a result of the tortures.

In the midst of the suffering, religion became a source of solace, a shield against the pain and misery. Simple churches were built — usually attap-thatched structures. These churches were the focal point for the prisoners during their internment and there was always full attendance at Mass.

The replica chapel that was situated outside the Prison has been relocated to the Changi Chapel and Museum. The museum that was next to the Chapel that housed the many items collected and donated by ex-POWs has also relocated to the Changi Chapel and Museum.

POWs were packed into Changi Prison like sardines. Sanitation was poor and many health problems arose.

E1 Changi Prison

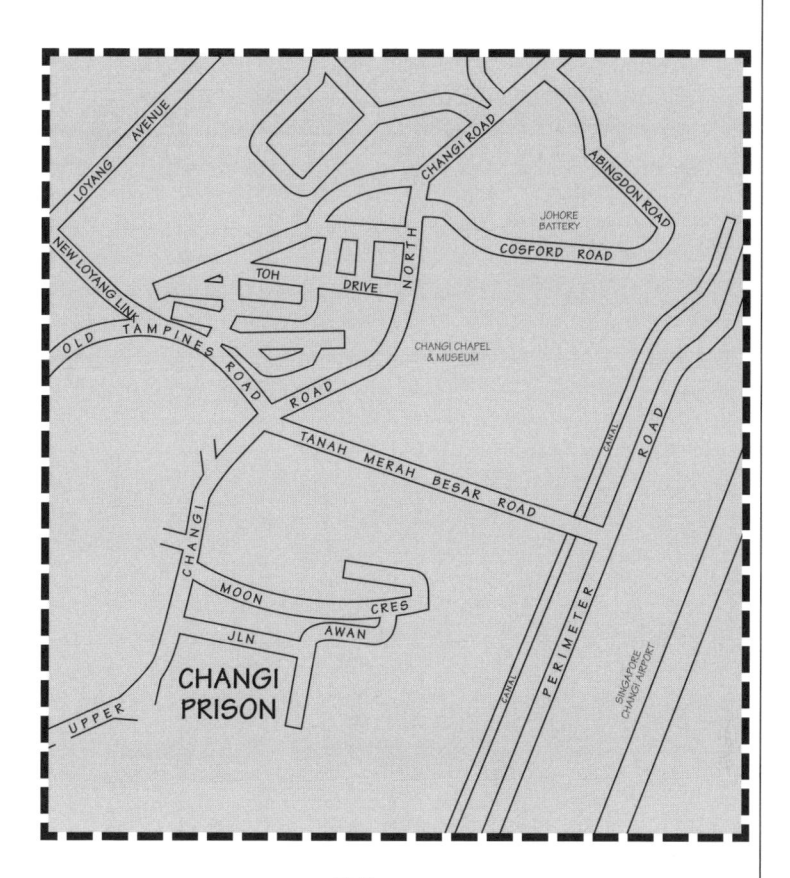

Notes

The Changi Chapel and Museum is located at 1000 Upper Changi Road North. On display are many items collected and donated by ex-POWs as well as a replica of the Changi Murals. It is open from 9.30 am to 4.30 pm daily. Admission is free.

Selarang Barracks

Many military POWs were imprisoned here during their three years of captivity. It was here that the famous Selarang Barracks Square Incident occurred in Sep 1942. Four young soldiers (Cpl. Rodney Breavington, Pte. Victor Gale, Pte. Harold Waters and Pte. Eric Fletcher) who tried to escape from prison were recaptured.

As a result, the Japanese wanted the POWs to sign a document promising not to escape under any circumstances. This was against the Geneva Convention on POWs which permitted opportunities of escape.

When the POWs refused, the Japanese crammed 15,400 men, including those brought over from Changi, into the barracks which was meant for only 1,200 men. The square was crowded with makeshift tents as men spilled out from the buildings.

There were no toilet facilities although each barracks building had about four to six toilets, which were flushed from small cisterns on the roofs. The Japanese, however, cut the water supply off and these toilets could not be used. The Japanese only allowed one tap to be used and prisoners had to line up in the early hours of the morning and that queue would go on all day. Each man was allowed one quart of water for drinking, washing and everything else.

To force the POWs to sign, the Japanese had the four soldiers shot on Changi beach on 2 Sep 1942 with senior POW officers watching. The various senior British commanders, under Col. E.B. Holmes, were taken to the Beting Kusah anti-aircraft practice ground near Selarang to witness the execution. The four men, one still in pyjamas, were lined up, three paces apart, with their backs to the sea. A firing squad faced them some 50 yards away. Cpl. Breavington pleaded in vain with the two Japanese officers present, Col. Makimura and Lt. Okasaki, to shoot him only as he alone was responsible. The gunners then knelt down and as the four prisoners saluted, four shots rang out. Cpl. Breavington cried out that he was only wounded and called to be finished off. The others were also not dead and further shots were fired into the bodies.

With the desperate food and sanitary conditions getting worse daily, and the threat of an epidemic breaking out in the overcrowded camp, the men were persuaded by their officers to sign the document to prevent any more unnecessary deaths. The signing took place on 5 Sep and after that the prisoners were returned to their original barracks.

After the war, on 7 Apr 1946, Maj. Gen. Shimpei Fukuei, the Japanese commander who ordered the execution, was executed at the same site. Nothing remains of the barracks now, except for the Officers' Mess, as the whole area has been redeveloped to house SAF troops. A poem by an unknown author (next page) bears witness to the fate of the four men.

Above: The POWs were all crammed at Selarang Barracks and many spilled out onto the square in makeshift tents. Because an epidemic threatened to break out, the POWs decided to sign the document rather than lose more lives.

Opposite Below: POWs signing the "No Escape" document.

THE CORPORAL AND HIS PAL

He stood, a dauntless figure
Prepared to meet his fate,
Upon his lips a kindly smile,
One arm about his mate,
His freed hand held a picture
Of the one he loved most dear,
And though the hand was trembling
It was not caused by fear.
No braver man e'er faced his death
Before a firing squad
Than stood that day upon the square
And placed his trust in God.
He drew himself up proudly
And faced the leering foe.
His ragged face grew stern: "I ask
One favour ere I go.
Grant unto me this last request
That's in your power to give,
For myself I ask no mercy
But let my comrade live."
Then turning to the guardhouse
Where his sad-faced Colonel stands
A witness to his pending fate
Brought here by Jap command.
He stiffened to attention
His hand swings up on high
To hat brim, in a swift salute.
"I'm ready now to die."
They murdered him in hatred
Prolonged his tortured end
In spite of all his pleadings
They turned and shot his friend.
They said he was example
Of what they had in store
For others who attempt escape
Whilst Prisoners of War.
Example, yes – of how to die,
And how to meet one's fate.
Example, true – of selfless love
A man has for his mate.
And when he reaches Heaven's Gate
The Angels will be nigh,
And welcome to their midst a man
Who knew the way to die.
Whilst here below in letters gold,
The scroll of fame e'er shall
The story tell of how they died,
A Corporal and his Pal.

E2 Selarang Barracks

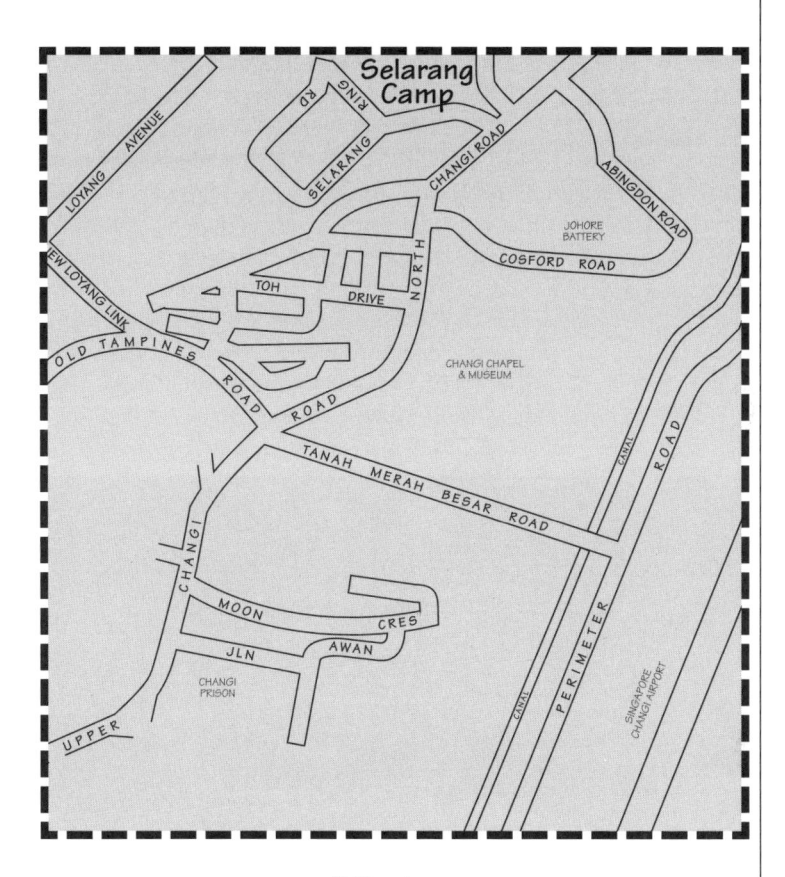

Notes

Selarang Barracks is now a camp of the Singapore Armed Forces. Although access is prohibited, a sign stands outside the camp's entrance recounting the sad occurrences in Selarang.

The Johore Battery

After World War I (1914–1918), the British realised that Japanese naval power was expanding and posed a potential threat. In view of the emergence of Japan as a power to reckon with in the Far East, it became imperative for the British to develop Singapore as a Naval Base. Sembawang on the Johore Straits was the chosen site of the new naval base. At that time, the British were certain any attack on Singapore would come from the sea, and as the entire defence strategy was built around Britain's naval power, coastal defences had to be put in place to protect Singapore from any attack by sea. Some major coastal batteries were the Pasir Laba Battery, Labrador Battery, Fort Siloso Battery, Silingsing, Serapong and Connaught Batteries.

In the eastern parts, Changi was chosen as the base for the Royal Artillery batteries under the Changi Fire Command. They comprised

The Eastern Tour

six batteries of 15-inch, 9.2-inch and 6-inch weapons sited at the eastern entrance to the Johore Straits to guard against any attack on the Naval Base from the east. Of these, the 15-inch battery located in the remote Bee Hoe area was to be the main artillery battery. Work began at a feverish pace at first to fortify the area, but soon had to stop due to budget cuts in Britain. At a time when Japanese ambitions were becoming more apparent, the Sultan of Johore donated £500,000 as a Silver Jubilee Gift for King George V in 1935. Of this, £400,000 was used to finance the installation of two of the three 15-inch guns in Bee Hoe. The last of the guns was mounted in 1938. This group of three 15-inch guns and their installations were named the Johore Battery in acknowledgement of the Sultan's contribution.

The 15-inch guns at the Johore Battery were also known as Monster Guns, so called because of their sheer size. At the start of World War II, they were the biggest and heaviest pieces of coastal artillery in the British Empire and were capable of piercing the armour of the most powerful battleships at that time. Some three storeys below the gun emplacement is a labyrinth of tunnels that was used to store ammunition to support the three monster guns. Before the British surrendered, orders were sent out to destroy the guns to prevent them from falling into enemy hands. The tunnels were sealed up after the war.

Opposite Below: *An outline of the complex tunnel system of the Battery.*

Left: *The replica 15-inch gun at the Battery.*

Page 104: *One of the tunnels at the Battery.*

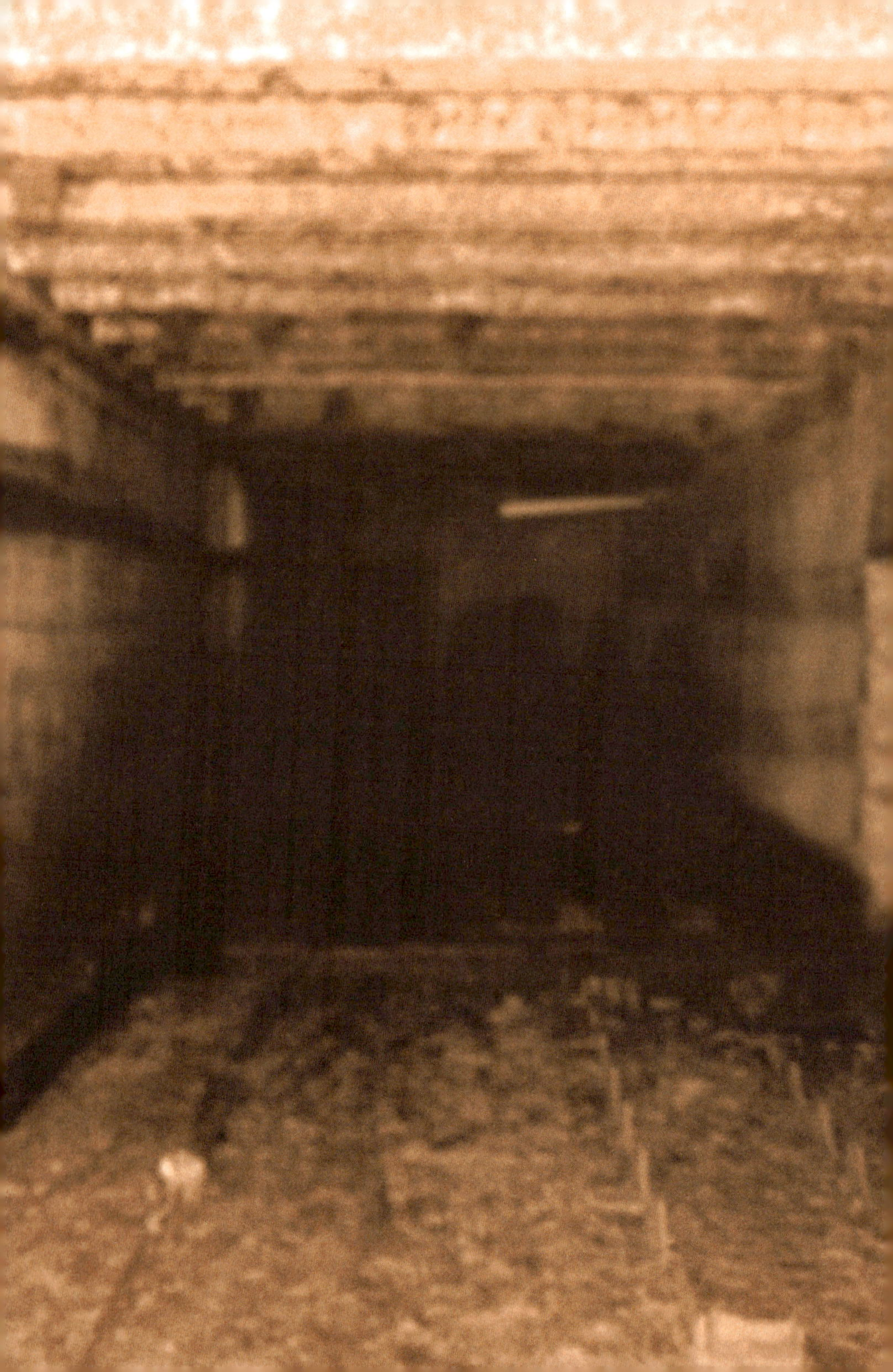

E3 The Johore Battery

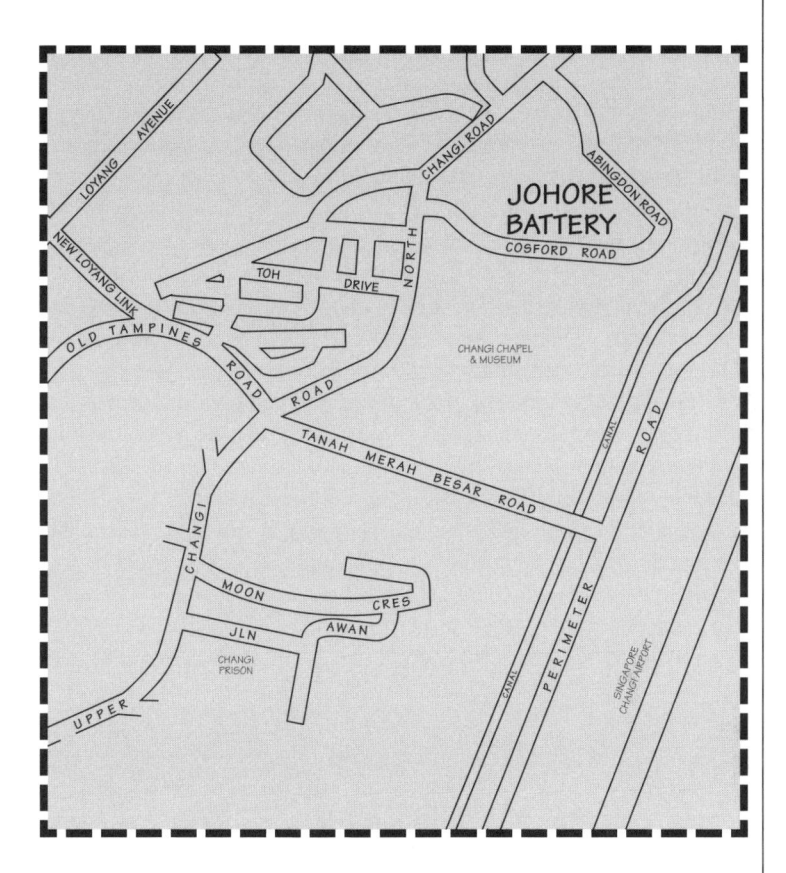

Notes

The Johore Battery with its labyrinth of tunnels was first discovered in Apr 1991 by the Prisons Department during routine cleaning at its Abingdon Centre. At the site, visitors can see a replica of the monster gun as well as view the tunnel network at ground level. Described as the most significant war discovery in recent history, the Johore Battery can be found at Cosford Road, Changi. Entry is free of charge and unrestricted.

Changi Murals

During the Occupation, Changi Camp was used as a military POW camp. It was also used as a hospital for the prisoners. A few blocks, including Blk 151, were allocated to dysentery patients. The left corner of the ground floor of Blk 151 was converted into St Luke's Chapel by the Rev F.H. Stallard. Many sick and dying soldiers sought spiritual strength and refuge here.

Among them was a British soldier called Stanley Warren, a bombardier of No. 15 Field Regiment. While he was recovering from his illness, he was inspired to paint a set of biblical murals. Since paint was not easily available, he had to mix his own colours from many different sources. His fellow prisoners willingly helped him to scout for dyes and other materials from which the paint was made. He put different faces on his characters in the murals, so as to add a touch of realism. Warren was painting the Nativity mural just before Christmas when he came down with dysentery. Warren's sickness was also complicated by stones in his kidney. He was only just able to complete the murals before he became too sick to move. However, as he lay sick in his bed, he could hear the Christmas Mass and felt glad that he had been able to contribute somewhat to their Christmas at Changi.

151

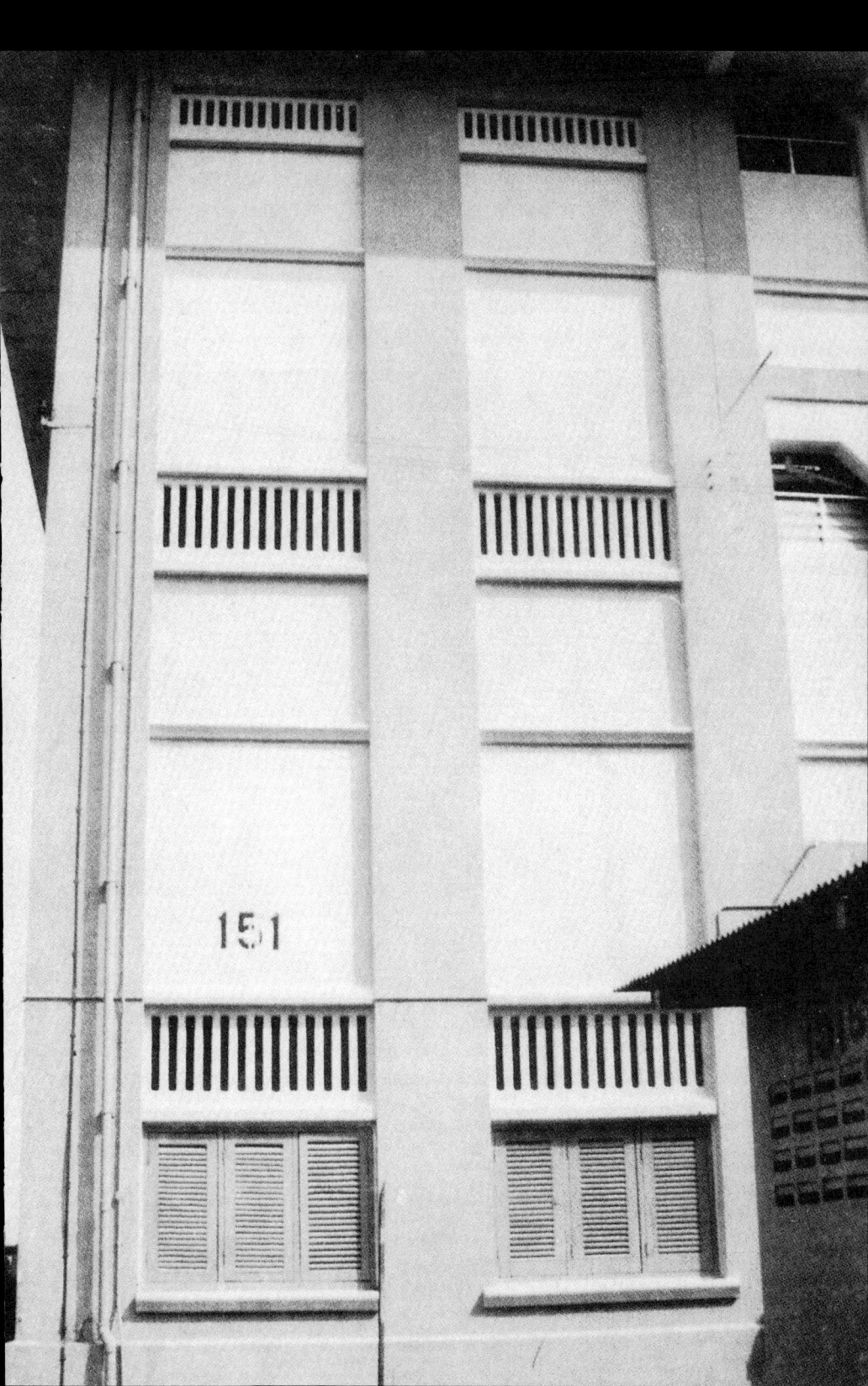

Page 107: Blk 151 stands as a solemn reminder as to how faith can overcome even the worst of times.

Page 106 and Below: Faith inspired Stanley Warren to paint the murals. Although he was suffering from an illness, his contribution helped to make life a little more bearable for others.

There were originally five life-sized murals but the Japanese destroyed a wall when they extended one of the rooms. Now only four and one-quarter murals remain.

After the Japanese surrender, the murals were forgotten until 1958 when the Royal Air Force discovered traces of colour on the walls whilst cleaning out the storeroom. A search began in the U.K. for the POW who painted them. A year later, Warren was found and was persuaded to come back in Dec 1963 to restore his murals. He made two more trips back — in Jul 1982 and May 1988 for restoration works.

Today, the murals stand as a reminder of the suffering and courage of the POWs in Changi.

E4 Changi Murals

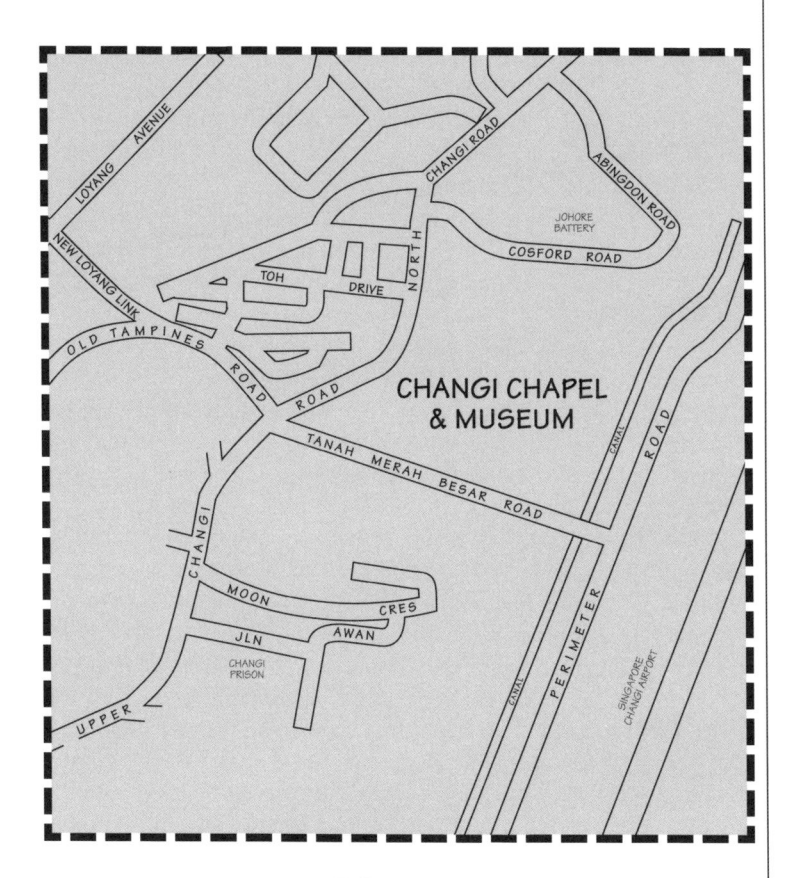

Notes

Access to the Murals is restricted as they are located within a Singapore Armed Forces Camp. Visitors can view a replica of the Murals at the Changi Chapel and Museum located at 1000 Upper Changi Road North.

Fortress Singapore

OTHER MEMORIALS

The Lim Bo Seng Memorial was unveiled at the Esplanade on 29 June 1954.

Lim Bo Seng's Memorial During the war, many locals volunteered their services to the British to resist the Japanese advancement to Malaya. One of them was Lim Bo Seng. Lim's sentiment against anti-Japanese aggression was first displayed during the 1937 Sino-Japanese war when he helped to raise money for the China Relief fund. Later, as Head of the Labour Services Corps, he provided thousands of labourers to the British in their war effort against the Japanese.

Two days before Singapore surrendered, he was persuaded to depart. Lim landed on a small Indonesian island where he joined a party of British military personnel. Together, they left for Sumatra, enroute to India. In Calcutta, Lim Bo Seng met Lt. Col. Goodfellow, Richard Broome and John Davis, who were key members of Force 136, a part of the Special Operation Executive (SOE) set up by the British to stimulate the support of local resistance movements in enemy occupied territories.

Lim assisted the British in getting the Chinese Nationalist government's support for Force 136. He later assumed the command of Force 136's Malayan Chinese Section and was actively involved in recruiting agents and training them in the jungle. In May 1943, Force 136 launched the first of a series of operations to infiltrate Japanese occupied Malaya via submarine. In Nov 1943, Lim left Ceylon for Malaya as Leader of Ops Gustavus V. While in Ipoh, Lim was warned of the danger there but he refused to leave without warning his men of the situation. They were arrested in March 1944 after the Japanese Kempeitai was tipped off by an MPAJA element, Lai Teck.

Lim and his men were jailed at Batu Gajah prison. Although tortured, Lim refused to divulge the names of members of Force 136. After three months of torture, malnutrition and deliberate lack of medical attention for his illness, Lim died in prison on 29 June 1944 at the age of 34.

After the war, Lim's remains were brought back to Singapore by the British and buried at MacRitchie Reservoir with full military honours. On 29 June 1954, Lim Bo Seng's memorial was unveiled at the Esplanade. His martyrdom so impressed the Chinese Nationalist Government that they issued a citation commending him for his services. He was also posthumously awarded

Other Memorials

the rank of Major-General. The Lim Bo Seng Memorial still stands today in memory of the man who epitomises the time-honoured spirit of patriotism and self-sacrifice.

Japanese Cemetery Park The Japanese Cemetery Park at Chuan Hoe Avenue (near Seletar) houses several graves of World War II Japanese soldiers. Among these graves is a prominent tombstone where the ashes of the Japanese Commander-in-Chief of the Southern Army, Field Marshall Count Hisaichi Terauchi, were buried. Terauchi was too ill to surrender at the City Hall to Lord Louis Mountbatten, the Supreme Allied Commander of the Southeast Asian Command, on 12 Sep 1945. He sent his family sword to Lt. Gen. Itagaki who surrendered on behalf of the Japanese. Terauchi was placed under house arrest and died of a stroke on 12 June 1946 at Johor Bahru.

Another tombstone marks the location where the ashes of 135 Japanese soldiers executed for war crimes are buried, along with those of 79 others. Also buried at the Japanese Cemetery Park are the ashes of Japanese soldiers that had previously been placed at Shonan Churieto as well as the ashes of Japanese civilians, including the women companions of Japanese soldiers during the Occupation years.

The final resting place of Field Marshall Count Hisaichi Terauchi, Japanese Commander-in-Chief of the Southern Army, at the Japanese Cemetery.

111

Members of the Krait committee unveiling the plaque commemorating Operation Jaywick and Rimau at the remembrance ceremony on 28 Sep 1993.

Operation Jaywick and Rimau In the early morning hours of 27 Sep 1943, Keppel Harbour was rocked by a series of explosions that eventually destroyed a total of seven ships. The daring attack threw the Japanese into great confusion. A thorough search was made on the surrounding islands of Singapore but no trace of the saboteurs was ever found.

This successful sabotage mission was carried out by members of the Z Special Force operating from Australia. Using an old Japanese vessel (named "*Krait*"), 14 members of Z Force made a daring raid on the shipping lines of Keppel Harbour under the code name of "Operation Jaywick". From a tiny island at the southern end of the Riau Archipelago, three teams of two canoeists each set out from *Krait*, canoed into Keppel Harbour and attached magnetic explosive limpet-mines to seven ships.

Following the successful Jaywick operation, another attempt was made to infiltrate the Japanese lines in Oct 1944. This second attempt — Operation Rimau — failed after the team was discovered by the Japanese on the Riau Archipelago islands. In the ensuing chase, 13 men were killed and 10 brought back to Singapore, where they stood trial and were executed on 7 July 1945. Six members of this operation were from Jaywick. Before they were executed, the 10 men were held in high esteem by their captors for their courage and bravery and were treated extremely well during their captivity.

In remembrance of these brave men, a plaque was placed at the former World Trade Centre amphitheatre by the Australian Krait Committee on 28 Sep 1993.

Other Memorials

The Civilian War Memorial Located in the War Memorial Park at Beach Road, it is dedicated to the civilians of all races who were victims of the Japanese Occupation of Singapore (1942–1945). Amongst these victims were the many Chinese men taken away during the "Sook Ching" or Screening Operation. This operation was conducted by the Japanese to remove undesirable elements in Singapore. It is believed that between 5,000 and 50,000 Chinese were massacred by the Japanese.

The need for a memorial arose when a large number of remains belonging to civilian victims of the Occupation were unearthed in Feb 1962 in areas like Siglap, Changi and Bukit Timah. The Singapore Chinese Chamber of Commerce (SCCC) undertook this responsibility to gather these remains from all over the island and to find a place to bury them as a token of remembrance.

On 13 Mar 1963, then Prime Minister Lee Kuan Yew, set aside the present piece of land for the building of a memorial dedicated to civilians killed in WWII. The SCCC set up a Memorial Building Fund Committee and with the support of the Government and the local population, plans began for the construction of the Memorial.

An open competition was held for the design of the Memorial and it was awarded to the architectural firm of Swan and Maclaren. One of the characteristics of the Memorial is its height of 61 metres and its four columns. The columns, representing the four races, are joined together at the base — signifying the unity of the races.

On 23 Apr 1966, construction works began and the Memorial was completed in Jan 1967.

On 15 Feb 1967, the Memorial was officially unveiled by then Prime Minister Lee Kuan Yew who laid a wreath on behalf of the Government and the people of Singapore. Religious rites were conducted by officials of the Inter-Religious Organisation[1] and a three-minute silence was observed in honour of the dead. Those present included the victims' families, members of the diplomatic corps (including the Japanese Ambassador), religious chiefs and representatives from the four races.

Each year on 15 Feb, memorial services are conducted at the Memorial. This service is open to all.

---

[1]The Inter-Religious Organisation (IRO) is the only inter-faith organisation in Singapore for promoting peace and harmony among the various religions. The IRO General Assembly comprises members from the nine religions — Hinduism, Judaism, Zoroastrianism, Buddhism, Taoism, Christianity, Islam, Sikhism and Baha'i.

The Cenotaph Located at the Esplanade, the Cenotaph was initially erected as a memorial to those who gave their lives in WWI. However, it later included those who died in WWII as well.

The memorial was designed by the famous architectural firm of Swan and Maclaren. This firm was also responsible for the design of the Civilian War Memorial. The foundation stone for the Cenotaph was laid on 15 Nov 1920 by Sir Lawrence Nunns Guillemard, the Governor of the Straits Settlements.

On 31 Mar 1922, it was unveiled by the Prince of Wales during his tour of Malaya, India, Australia and New Zealand. Accompanying him was young Lord Louis Mountbatten. Admiral Lord Mountbatten was to return to Singapore later as the Supreme Allied Commander, Southeast Asia Command. It was Admiral Lord Mountbatten who accepted the Japanese surrender at City Hall (the building opposite the Cenotaph) on 12 Sep 1945.

WWII PLAQUES AND HISTORIC SITES

The old Cathay building.

Cathay Building Built in 1939, Cathay Building was the then tallest building in Singapore, housing a cinema, offices and the Malaya Broadcasting Corporation. Before the British surrendered to the Japanese, Cathay was one of the buildings where hundreds of British army deserters sought refuge from the constant Japanese aerial and artillery bombardment. The roof of Cathay was also used to spot enemy guns. Crowds gathered at the Cathay Building on 9 Feb 1942 for the official evacuation from Singapore.

When the British surrendered on 15 Feb 1942, a large Japanese flag was displayed on top of the Cathay Building, as requested by Lt. Col. Suchita of the Japanese General Staff, to signify to the Japanese that Gen. Percival had accepted their condition of ceasefire and that he was on his way to meet Gen. Yamashita. The flag was displayed for only ten minutes for fear of incidents on the part of the Allied soldiers.

After the surrender, five heads of looters were displayed in front of the Cathay Building by the Japanese authority to deter looting. The Cathay Building was taken over by the Japanese military and became the office of its Propaganda Division. Media services such as newspapers and radios were controlled. Programmes aired were those considered suitable, such as appreciation of the Japanese language, Japanese songs and weekly news and commentaries. Mandarin, Malay and Hindi were used in the broadcast. English was also occasionally used to teach the Japanese language.

In 1945, Admiral Lord Louis Mountbatten made his headquarters at the Cathay Building when he arrived in Singapore to accept the Japanese surrender.

Old YMCA Building The old YMCA Building was opened in Jan 1911 and served as a venue for youth activities. During the Japanese Occupation, it became the headquarters of the East District Branch of the much feared Kempeitai (the Japanese Military Police). The Kempeitai was responsible for crushing resistance to Japanese rule. It wielded almost absolute power and could arrest and punish at will. Heads of looters were displayed outside the old YMCA Building and the Cathay Building to deter looting.

During the Feb 1942 Sook Ching Operation to eliminate anti-Japanese elements among the Chinese, many were arrested on mere suspicion of anti-Japanese activities. At the Kempeitai Headquarters, suspects were interrogated and tortured. Screams of tortured victims could be heard emanating from the building. During the "Double Tenth" incident in Oct 1943, the Japanese arrested and interrogated many civilians, including 57 internees of the Changi Internment Camp, suspected of helping in a sabotage mission to blow up seven Japanese oil tankers.

The old YMCA Building was one of the venues where suspects were interned, interrogated and tortured. The common methods of tortures included the use of water and electric shock treatment, caning and burning with cigarette butts. The old YMCA building was demolished in 1981.

The Old YMCA building, used by the Japanese Kempeitai, witnessed many scenes of horror as the Japanese forced confessions from their victims using various methods of torture.

Indian National Army Monument The Indian National Army (INA) was formed with Japanese support in Sep 1942. The INA's aim was to fight for the liberation of India from British rule. Not all Indians joined the INA but it gained widespread support under the leadership of Subhas Chandra Bose.

Bose arrived in Singapore in July 1943 to assume the leadership of the independence movement. He was a compelling leader with great flair of speech and the movement flourished under his guidance. On 8 July 1945, Bose laid a foundation stone in the vicinity of the Cenotaph in dedication to the Indian independence movement. Inscribed on it were the words "Ittifaq", "Ithmad" and "Kurbani", meaning unity, faith and sacrifice. The memorial was destroyed with the return of the British at the end of the war in Sep 1945. When the Japanese surrendered on 15 Aug 1945, Bose flew to Saigon and was killed in an airplane crash on 18 Aug 1945.

Subhas Chandra Bose inspecting the Rani of Jhansi Regiment, the women's regiment of the INA. The regiment was commanded by Cpt. (Dr.) Lakshi, seen accompanying Bose. The INA took part in a combined Indian-Japanese offensive on the Burmese front in March 1944. However, the initial successes in the Burma campaign were followed by demoralising defeats under the British. The campaign was abandoned in July 1944.

7 Adam Park Situated along Adam Road, this house was the Headquarters of the 1st Battalion, Cambridgeshire Regiment. This regiment defended the Adam Park housing estate against the invading Japanese army in Feb 1942. It is now used by the National University of Singapore Society.

Tanglin Officers' Mess Located at Tanglin Road, this mess was used by officers of the British garrison stationed at Tanglin Barracks. During WWII, Tanglin Barracks served as the Headquarters of Major-General Gordon Bennett, Commander of the Australian Imperial Forces. After the war, Tanglin Barracks was used by the British as the General Headquarters of the Far East Land Forces. The Ministry of Foreign Affairs now occupies this building.

Pulau Sejahat Located opposite Pulau Tekong, Pulau Sejahat is an island dedicated to the WWII defence of the northeastern waterway access to Singapore. It is an example of the British seaward defence efforts and technology of that time.

Pasir Panjang Machine-Gun Pillbox This pillbox probably formed part of the defence line at Pasir Panjang and was quite likely used by the Malay Regiment in the defence of Pasir Panjang Ridge against advancing Japanese forces.

Sime Road Pillbox Located at Sime Road opposite the Golf Course, this pillbox was probably used in the defence of the area and the Combined Army and Air Force Operational Headquarters which was sited in the vicinity.

Beach Road Police Station During the Japanese Occupation, some Chinese, Indians and Jews were held here before being sent to Changi.

Havelock Road Internment Camp This camp was mainly a civilian camp housing about 5,000 internees. Internees from this camp were sent to work all over Singapore.

Sime Road Camp Site Located along Sime Road, this camp was one of the many POW camps set up in Singapore. Internees from here were used to build the Japanese Syonan Jinja shrine at MacRitchie Reservoir.

WWII Plaques and Historic Sites

Syonan Jinja This Japanese Shrine was built by the internees from the Sime Road POW camp. It was dedicated to the Japanese soldiers who died in the battle for Singapore. Not much remains of the shrine except for some remnants and the steps leading up to the shrine.

Changi Beach Massacre Site Located at Changi Beach Park, this was the site where many Chinese were massacred by the Japanese during the infamous "Sook Ching" operation.

Punggol Beach Massacre Site Located at Punggol Point, this is another site where many Chinese were massacred by the Japanese during the infamous "Sook Ching" operation.

Sentosa Beach Massacre Site Located at Sentosa's Serapong Golf Course, this site was where British soldiers buried the bodies of Chinese civilians that had washed up on the beach. These victims were taken out to sea and shot by the Japanese.

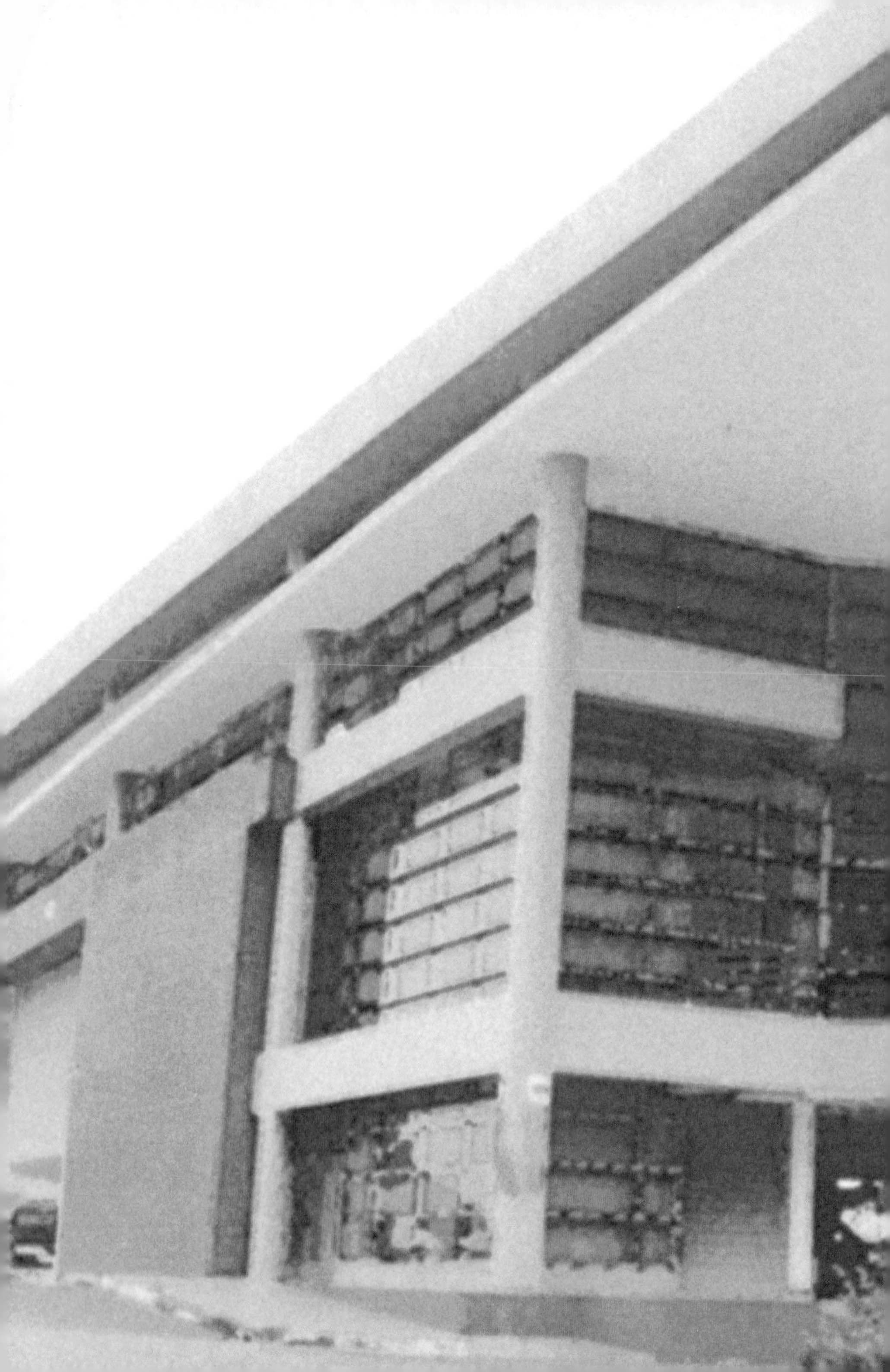

THE MILITARY MUSEUMS

Fortress Singapore

RSN Museum

The Naval Museum of the Republic of Singapore Navy is housed in the Endurance Block in Sembawang Camp. Officially opened in 1987, the museum features a collection of souvenirs and mementoes to record the navy's history. In it are pictures, documents, naval uniforms, weapons, models of military vessels and other artifacts that date back to the formation of the Straits Settlements Royal Naval Volunteer Reserve in 1934. It traces the growth of the navy from its volunteer days to the formation of the Maritime Command in 1968 and, later, its transformation into the RSN.

As you walk through the museum, you will be able to see many photographs illustrating the significant events that have occurred in the RSN. Showcases of old medals, badges and rank insignias which are of great historical value are displayed.

Visitors can view a large collection of memento plaques received from different countries on friendly visits to the navy. You can also get to see models of the various ships of the RSN, both old and new with brief descriptions of their capabilities. Models of the Harpoon and Gabriel missile and a torpedo are also on exhibition. Other attractions include a mine sweeping hammer, parvane floats, 20mm Oerlikon guns, 40mm Bofor guns, a decompression chamber, a boat mast, and even the original Horsburgh Lighthouse reflector.

Maritime Memories

M1 RSN Museum

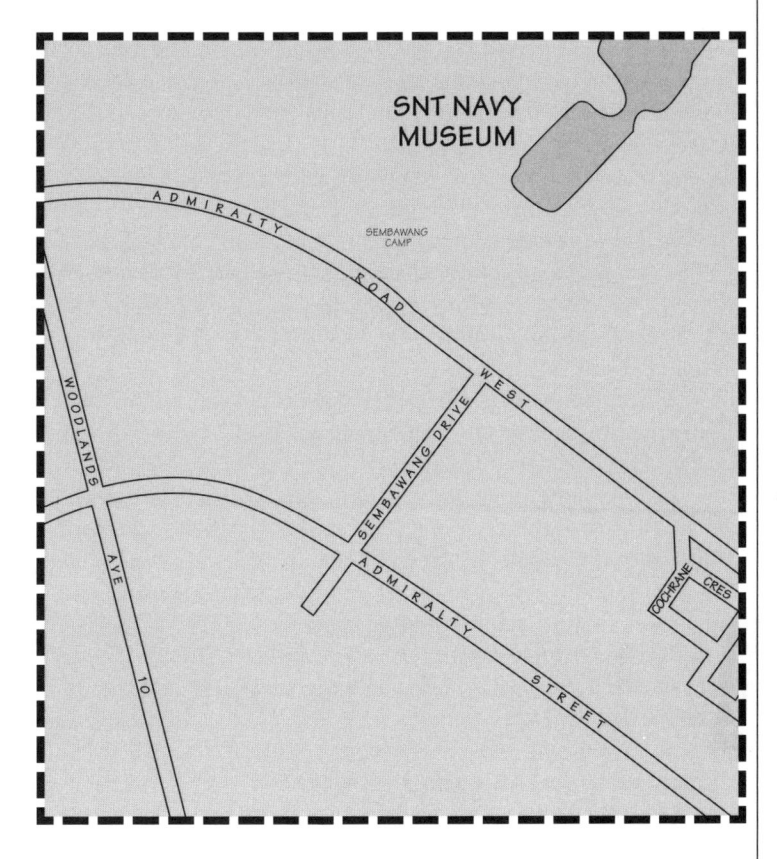

Notes

The Museum is open daily except Sundays from 8.30 am to 5.00 pm on weekdays and from 8.30 am to 1.00 pm on Saturdays. Admission is free.

Fortress Singapore

RSAF Museum

The Air Force Museum was first established in 1988 in Changi. It underwent a second stage development and expansion two years later. It was relocated to Paya Lebar and was officially opened on 22 Mar 2001.

The museum resides on 10,600m^2 of land with a total built-up area of 4,600m^2. The exhibition area comprises an outdoor gallery, the "History of Aviation" gallery on the first level and eight indoor galleries on the second level. The museum essentially captures the dramatic transformation of the Republic of Singapore Air Force (RSAF) from a fledgling air force to what it is today — a sophisticated and professional air force.

The theme for the entire display is "Men, Machines and Methods." It tells the story of an RSAF that is dynamic and forward looking; always at the frontier of technology — a First Class Air Force. The museum showcases the interface between "Men, Machines and Methods" through the proud display of the RSAF's heritage. A special feature of the museum is the integrated use of information technology to enhance the exhibits. The e-mail kiosks located at the concourse and atrium allow visitors to register as guests and get connected to international air force museums and aviation sites. Through a readily packaged network of hyperlinks, visitors can also surf these sites from the comfort of their homes and even share these sites with friends and relatives. Through this innovation, the museum hopes to promote greater interest in aviation and aviation history.

Flying High

Military Museums

One of the museum's proud exhibits, the Bloodhound missile.

Opposite Below: *Outdoor exhibits at the Museum.*

M2 RSAF Museum

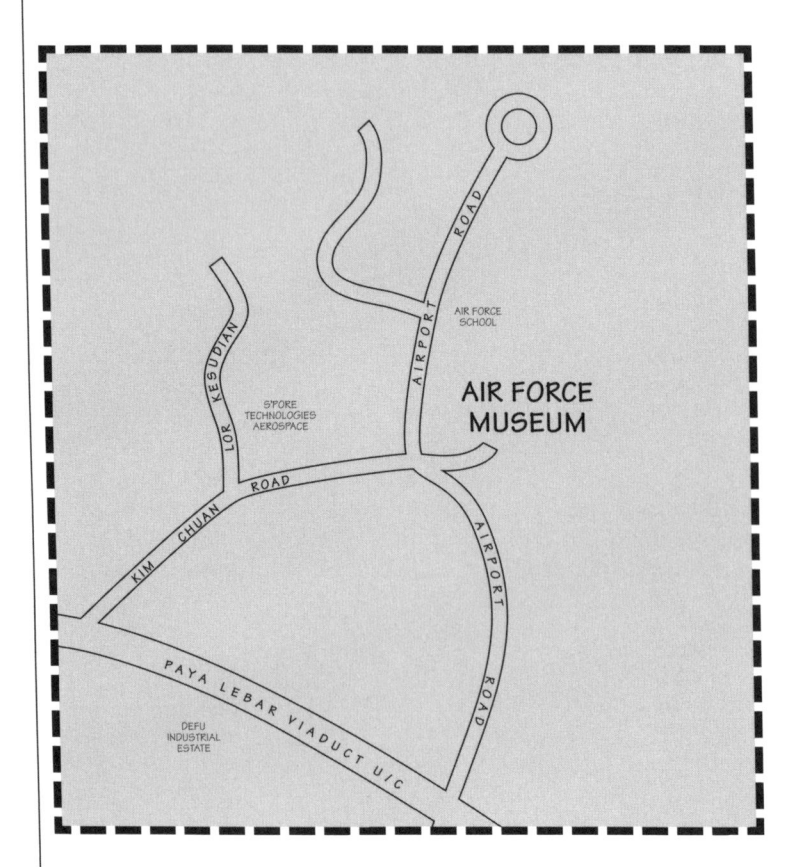

Notes

The Museum is open from Tuesdays to Sundays from 8.30 am to 5.00 pm. It is closed on Mondays and public holidays. Admission is free.

Selected Bibliography

SELECTED BIBLIOGRAPHY

WWII Books on the Battle for Singapore and Malaya (Some of the following were used for the compilation of this book.)

A Battle To Be Remembered: Oral History Extracts of War-Time Singapore. Editor, Tan Beng Luan – Singapore: Oral History Department, 1988.

Abdul Wahab. *Medical Students During The Japanese Invasion of Singapore, 1941–1942.* Edited by Cheah Jin Seng. Singapore: Academy of Medicine, 1987.

Allen, Louis. *Singapore 1941–1942.* London: Davis-Poynter, 1977.

Aspinall, George. *Changi Photographer: George Aspinall's Record of Captivity.* ABC Enterprises and William Collins P/L 1984.

Bailey, Douglas. *We Built And Destroyed.* London: Hurst and Blackett, 1944.

Barber, Noel. *Sinister Twilight: The Fall And Rise Again of Singapore.* London: Readers Union, 1969.

Brooke, Geoffrey. *Singapore's Dunkirk.* London: Copper, 1989.

Callahan, Raymond. *Worst Disaster: The Fall of Singapore.* Newark: University of Delaware Press, 1977.

Caffrey, Kate. *Out In The Midday Sun: Singapore 1941–1945.* London: Andre Deutsch, 1974.

Chua Ser Koon. *Malayan Chinese Resistance To Japan 1937–1945.* Cultural & Historical Publishing House Pte Ltd, 1984.

Connell, Brian. *Return Of The Tiger.* London: Evans, 1960.

Corr, Gerald H. *War Of The Springing Tigers.* London: Osprey, 1975.

Crisp, Dorothy. *Why We Lost Singapore.* London: D.Crisp, 1944.

Danaraj, T.J. *Japanese Invasion Of Malaya and Singapore: Memoirs Of A Doctor.* Kuala Lumpur: T.J. Danaraj, 1990.

Donnison, F.S.V. *British Military Administration In The Far East 1943 – 46.* London: H.M.S.O, 1956.

Draper, Alfred. *Storm Over Singapore.* London: W.H. Allen, 1987.

Falk, Stanley L. *Seventy Days To Singapore: The Malayan Campaign, 1941–1942.* London: Hale, 1975.

Gough, Richard. *SOE Singapore 1941–1942.* London: Kimber 1985.

Grenfell, Russell. *Main Fleet to Singapore.* Singapore: Oxford University Press, 1987.

Hall, Timothy. *The Fall Of Singapore.* North Ryde (NSW): Methuen Australia, 1983.

Harrison, Kenneth. *Brave Japanese.* Adelaide: Rigby, 1966.

Harrison, Kenneth. *Road To Hiroshima.* Rev. ed. Adelaide: Rigby, 1983.

Holmes, Richard. *The Bitter End.* Chichester: Anthony Bird Publications, 1982.

Hsia Zoh-Tsung. *Bitter Cup.* Singapore: University Education Press, 1974.

Huxtable, Charles. *From The Somme To Singapore: A Medical Officer In Two World Wars.* Turnbridge Wells; Costello, 1987.

Images Of War (10): Fall of Singapore. London: Marshall Cavendish, 1988.

Kennedy, J (Joseph). *When Singapore Fell: Evacuations And Escapes.* Basingstoke: Macmillan, 1989.

Kirby, S. Woodburn. *Singapore: The Chain Of Disaster.* London: Cassell, 1971.

Lewis, T.P.M. *Changi, The Lost Years: A Malayan Diary, 1941–1945.* Kuala Lumpur: Malayan Historical Society, 1984.

Lim, Janet. *Sold for Silver: An Autobiography.* Singapore: Oxford University Press, 1985.

127

Lim Thean-soo. *Destination Singapore (From Shanghai To Singapore)*. Singapore: Pan Pacific Book Distributors, 1976.

Lodge, A.B. *The Fall Of Gordon Bennett*. Sydney: Allen & Unwin, 1986.

Low, N.I. *This Singapore: Our City Of Dreadful Night*. City Book Store, 1946.

Low, N.I. *When Singapore Was Syonan-To*. Singapore: Times Editions, 1973.

Media Masters' World War II. *The Japanese Conquest Of Malaya and Singapore, December 1941–February 1942*.

MacGregor, Gordon Scott. *No Other Medicine*. Falmouth, Cornwall: G.S. MacGregor; 1984.

Menon, K.R. *East Asia In Turmoil: Letters To My Son*. Singapore Educational Publications Bureau, 1981.

Montgomery, Brian. *Shenton Of Singapore: Governor And Prisoner of War*. Singapore: Times Books International, 1984.

Moore, Michael. *Battalion At War: Singapore 1942*. Norwich: Gliddon, 1988.

Nelson, David. *The Story Of Changi Singapore*. Australia: Changi Publication Co, 1974.

Nelson, Hank. *P.O.W. Prisoners Of War: Australians Under Nippon*. Sydney: ABC Enterprises For Australia Broadcasting Corporation, 1985.

Okumiya, Masatake and Horikoshi, Jiro. *ZERO!* Washington: Zenger Publishing Co., Inc., 1979.

Probert, H. A. *History Of Changi*. Prison Industries in Changi Prison.

Shinozaki, Mamoru. *Syonan—My Story: The Japanese Occupation Of Singapore*. Singapore: Asia Pacific Press, 1975.

Shinozaki, Mamoru. *My Wartime Experiences In Singapore*. Singapore: Institute of Southeast Asian Studies, 1973.

Singapore: An Illustrated History, 1941–1984. Information Division, Ministry of Culture.

Singapore And Beyond. Compiled and edited by Don Wall-East Hills: 2/20 Battalion Association Secretary, 1985.

Smyth, John, Sir. *Percival And The Tragedy Of Singapore*. London: Macdonald, 1971.

Swinson, Arthur. *Defeat In Malaya: The Fall Of Singapore*. New York: Ballantine Books Inc, 1970.

The Japanese Occupation: Singapore 1942–1945. Archives and Oral History Department — Singapore: Singapore News & Publications Ltd. 1985.

Trail, H.F. O.B. *Some Shape Of Beauty*. Kuala Lumpur: The Incorporated Society of Planters, 1986.

Tsuji, Masanobu. *Singapore, The Japanese Version*. Translated by M.E. Lake, edited by H.V. Howe. Singapore: Oxford University Press, 1988.

Van Cuylenburg. *Singapore Through Sunshine and Shadow*. Singapore: Heinemann Asia, 1982.

Wang, Wilson. *God's Deliverance In The Day Of Trouble*. Translated by C.M. Lau, Lexington, Mass.: W.Wang, 1962.

Whitelocke, Cliff. *Gunners In The Jungle*. Eastwood, N.S.W: The 2/15 Field Regiment Association, 1983.

Winston G. Ramsey. *After The Battle. Number 31*. Plaistow Press Magazines Ltd., London E153JA.

FORTRESS SINGAPORE
The Battlefield Guide

DEC 8, 1941 KOTA BAHRU

GONG KEDAH AIRFIELD

FORTRESS SINGAPORE

Feb 8 1942

The "Tiger of Malaya," Yamashita, stood on the rampart of the Sultan's palace and sized up the island across the Straits of Johore. On its fringes, he could see Australian and Indian infantrymen hurriedly setting up obstacles and digging trenches in a final, desperate stand.

Around him were scattered the debris of war and among them, the most awesome fighting machine ever: the Imperial Guards, and the 5th and 18th Division. The Japanese army had swept through the entire length of peninsular Malaya and crushed the British resolve in 60 days.

Ahead lies his prize, Singapore – bastion of the British Empire east of Suez. The island fortress will be a fitting present for the anniversary of the legendary Emperor Jimmu on Feb 11 1942.

The main attack would begin tonight, on the Kranji and Sarimbun rivers.

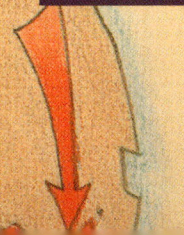

FORTRESS SINGAPORE
The Battlefield Guide

1942

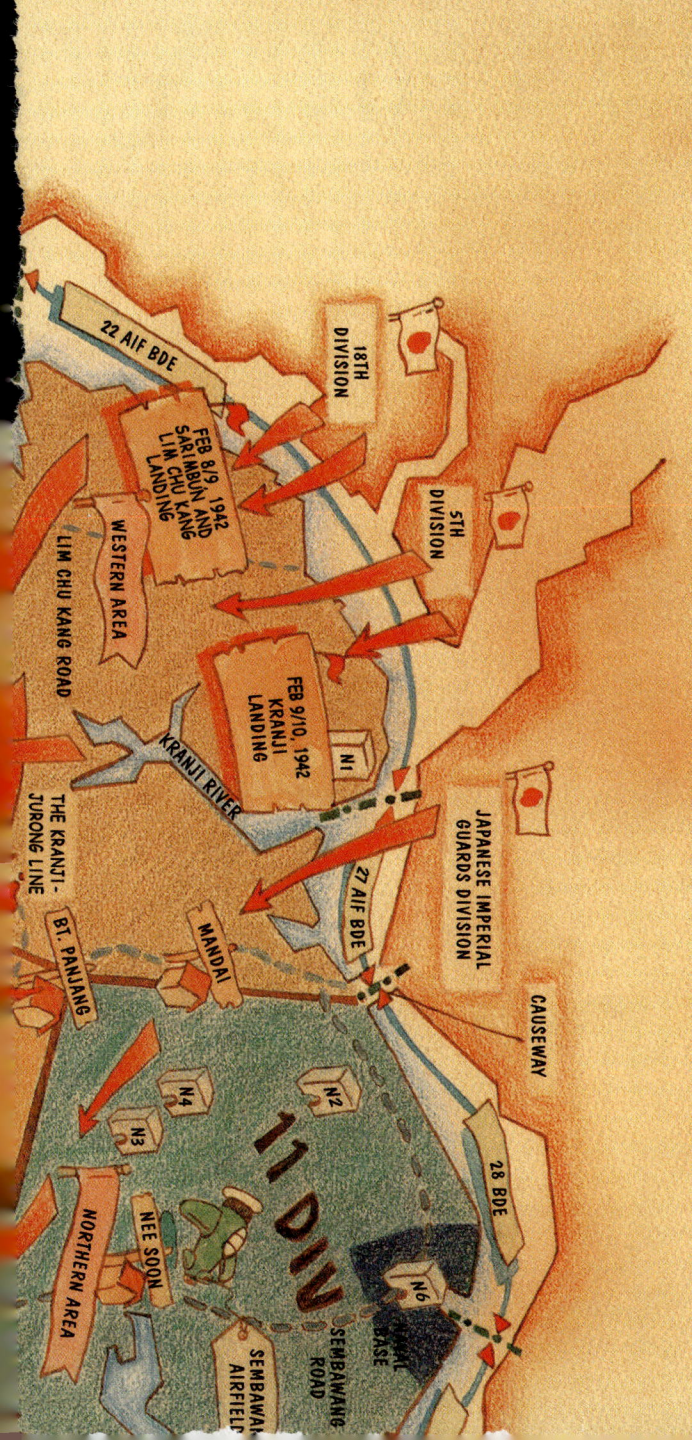

SINGAPORE

- 22 AIF BDE
- 18TH DIVISION
- FEB 8/9, 1942 SARIMBUN AND LIM CHU KANG LANDING
- 5TH DIVISION
- WESTERN AREA
- LIM CHU KANG ROAD
- FEB 9/10, 1942 KRANJI LANDING
- KRANJI RIVER
- N1
- THE KRANJI-JURONG LINE
- 27 AIF BDE
- JAPANESE IMPERIAL GUARDS DIVISION
- BT. PANJANG
- MANDAI
- CAUSEWAY
- N4
- N2
- N3
- 28 BDE
- 11 DIV
- NEE SOON
- NORTHERN AREA
- N6
- NAVAL BASE
- SEMBAWANG ROAD
- SEMBAWANG AIRFIELD

DEC 31, 1941
KUANTAN
DEC 10, 1941
JAPANESE AIRCRAFT
SINK
PRINCE OF WALES
JAPANESE AIRCRAFT
SINK
REPULSE
JAN 21, 1942
ENDAU
JAN 29, 1942
KLUANG
JAN 26, 1942
MERSING
JAN 28, 1942
JEMALUANG
JAN 31, 1942
JOHORE BAHRU
JAN 22, 1942
BATTLE OF
PARIT SULONG

A 1941 / 1942

JAN 7, 1942
SLIM RIVER

JAN 11, 19
KUALA LUM

JAN 16, 1942
MUAR

KEY:

→ Direction of Japanese Advance

✈ Airfield

● Where Fighting Took Place

MALAY

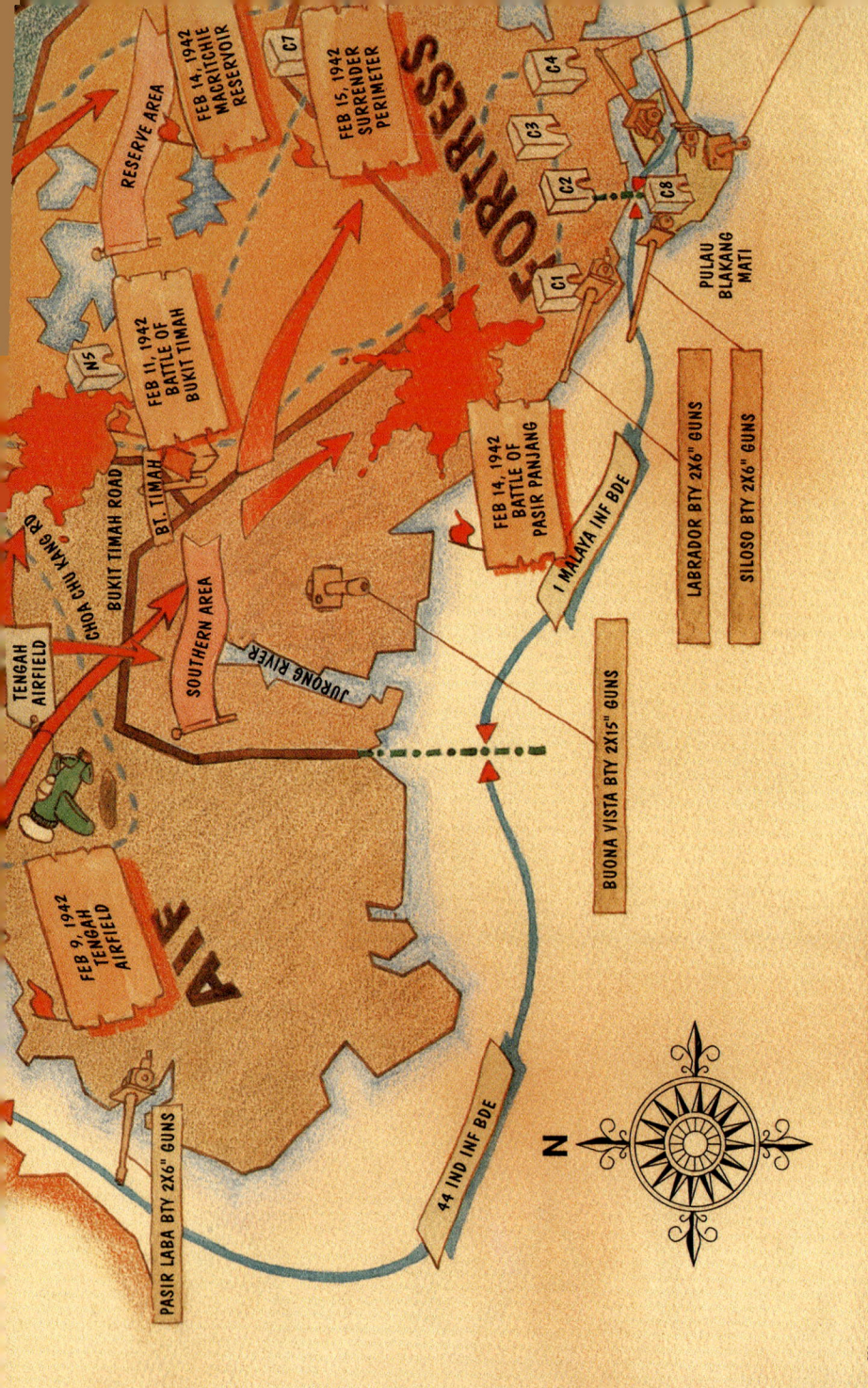

Illustration by *Eric Siow from AC Graphic*

TEKONG BTY 3X9.2" GUNS
SPHINX BTY 2X6" GUNS
JOHORE BTY 3X15" GUNS

2 MALAYA INF BDE

SOUTHERN AREA

TROOPS

KALLANG AIRFIELD

SERANGOON ROAD

SSVF BDE

SILINSING BTY 2X6" GUNS
SERAPONG BTY 2X6" GUNS
CONNAUGHT BTY 3X9.2" GUNS

KEY:

Area Boundaries in 1941
Brigade Boundaries in 1941
Main Roads

Direction of Japanese Advance

Airfield

Japanese Division

Where Fighting Took Place

Village

Battery

THE NORTHWESTERN TOUR
N1– Kranji Reservoir Park
N2– Sarimbun Beach Battle Site
N3– Kranji War Memorial
N4– Bukit Batok Hilltop
N5– Ford Motor Factory
N6– Bukit Timah Battle

THE EASTERN TOUR
E1– Changi Prison
E2– Selarang Barracks
E3– Johore Battery
E4– Changi Murals

THE CENTRAL TOUR
C1– Kent Ridge Park
C2– Labrador Park
C3– Alexandra Hospital
C4– Singapore General Hospital
C5– Padang & City Hall
C6– Kandahar Street
C7– Fort Canning Park
C8– Fort Siloso

MILITARY MUSEUMS
M1– RSN Museum
M2– RSAF Museum